SUCCESSFUL WRITING

Writers' Bookshop

SUCCESSFUL WRITING

**Inside information to give
you a headstart**

Teresa McCuaig

© Teresa McCuaig 1996

First published by Need2Know 1996
This edition published in 1997 by Writers' Bookshop,
7-11 Kensington High Street,
London W8 5NP

Edited by Kerrie Pateman
Typesetting by Forward Press Ltd

Contents

Introduction

According to recent statistics, thirty per cent of people in Britain say that they would like to become writers. That's a lot of competition. Does this statement discourage you? Don't worry; if you are convinced that you were born to write, not even the most pessimistic odds will be able to stop you. Books, magazines and newspapers are being published every day, and somebody has to provide the contents. It might as well be you!

Would-be writers come in all shapes and sizes. They range from children scribbling away in bed after 'lights out' to the teenager studying journalism at university. From the factory worker typing away in his spare time to the retired person hoping to supplement her pension income. From the unemployed person wanting to embark on a new career to the person who has managed to sell a few pieces but hopes to market more.

All these people have one thing in common; they not only write but they need to know how to sell their work. A question I'm often asked is this: is there a secret to getting published? Well, there aren't any secrets but there are important things you need to know, and that is what this book is all about.

While there are no guarantees in the writing business, careful preparation will help you to lessen the odds.

Let's suppose that you've written what you believe to be a fantastic article or a potentially best-selling novel. This is only the first step on the road to publication. Where do you send it? How do you know which magazine or publishing house will be a suitable home for your work? How do you get editors to look at it? Is it the required length or genre?

When your submission is accepted, what comes next? How much control do you have over your work? When should you not interfere with editorial decisions? How much will you be paid?

This book will answer many of your questions. It also lets you see things from the editor's side of the desk; many people come to the task with unreasonable expectations.

Alas, before the happy day arrives when you become a published writer, you will probably receive a number of rejection slips. Even the most famous writers have experienced this. Catherine Cookson, Beatrix Potter and Agatha Christie, all had their work turned down initially, yet today millions of their books are sold worldwide. They had this in common: each of them refused to give up.

We can help you turn rejection to your advantage. We can't promise that this book will turn you into a successful writer, but we do provide signposts along the way which, if noted carefully, will help you along the way. Reach for the stars!

1 GETTING STARTED

- How do I get started?
- Could you be a writer?
- The writing life
- Tools of the trade

We all have dreams. For many people, that dream involves becoming a professional writer, and not just someone who occasionally gets paid for writing, but a person who writes all the time and makes a living at it.

In many ways it's the ideal life. The writer doesn't have to battle the traffic on the way to work, he doesn't have to keep set hours and he can shut out the world and concentrate on the task at hand. It's a lonely existence in some ways, but when you're doing work that you love, who cares?

All you really need is a modicum of talent, a capacity for hard work, an appreciation of the rules of the craft and a lot of self-discipline. Some people insist that a great deal of talent is necessary 'The ability to write is inborn,' they say 'Either you have it, or you don't.' What they don't realise is that few successful writers are proficient in every form of the craft. While the author of best-selling fiction is obviously a born story teller she may be totally inept at crafting poetry, or interviewing people for a newspaper article.

The trick is to find your own niche. Some people know from the outset exactly what they wish to do; others choose to experiment with different media before they find their true vocation.

So why aren't more people successfully following a writing career? Probably because they don't stop to consider - and follow - the rules. By the time you reach the end of this book it will have been drummed into you several times that if you want your manuscript to be considered by an editor, you must follow certain guidelines.

In most spheres of life people understand the necessity for doing what is required of them in certain situations. What would we think of the footballer who deliberately scores goals for the opposition, or the sales rep who tries to sell biscuits to a clothing shop?

If these examples seem ridiculous, consider this: they are no more ludicrous than the writer who submits his article on motor cycle maintenance to a parenting magazine, or the author who tries to market a 12,000 word novel. The way to success is to learn the rules and stick to them.

How do I get started?

One of the questions most frequently posed by the novice writer is 'How do I get started?' Established writers receive old-fashioned looks when they respond with ' just do it,' but there really is no other answer. You must just sit down and write, whether it be letters to newspapers or an article on growing exotic vegetables. Use this book to learn the basics of the craft, but don't wait for inspiration to strike. If you hope to become a writer, the time to begin is now.

Another popular question, posed prematurely in most cases, is 'When should I leave my present job to take up writing as a full-time career?' Well, unless you have a private income, the answer is: don't think of it. Of course, if you've just received a million pound advance for the novel of the year, that's a different matter.

When I talk to high school pupils on Careers Day they look at me in disbelief when I tell them that yes, they should by all means write, but at the same time they should work at some other job which will bring in money. If they are lucky, this could be in a writing-related field such as journalism or public relations. This isn't what they want to hear. They want to go straight to the garret, typewriter in hand. They haven't yet come to grips with the world of rent money and food bills.

Perhaps it's different in your case. You've been in the work force for some years, you've been writing in your spare time, and you already have some published pieces to your credit. Couldn't you give up your day job now? Let me tell you a true story.

While working as an editor for a regional publishing house I received a book proposal and sample chapters from a previously unpublished writer. It seemed to be well done but it had to be turned down because we were no longer accepting unsolicited manuscripts. Apparently the young man hadn't consulted our listing in the various publishing directories, or he would have known this.

We were unable to return his material or let him know our decision because he hadn't enclosed the mandatory stamped, self addressed envelope. Publishers have enough difficulty making ends meet without shelling out money to return unsolicited submissions.

Somehow the young author managed to track me down at home (another no-no!).

'I hope you don't mind my phoning so late at night,' he said. 'I've been trying all evening but you're a hard person to get hold of.'

Remembering the kindly editor who shepherded me along when my first novel was going through the various stages of production, I resisted the urge to slam down the phone. Instead, I gently broke the bad news, passed on a few tips, and wished the author success in placing his book. Then he said 'I've been offered a really good job. Do you think I should take it? Or should I wait until my book is accepted and keep on writing instead?'

'Do both,' I said. 'Take the job and write in your spare time.'

He was obviously disappointed by this response, but it was good advice. It takes time for a book to sell. Then there is usually a gap between acceptance of a manuscript and any monetary return. Lucky first-time authors occasionally do receive six figure advances but this only happens when they have produced 'commercial' books which stand to bring huge returns for their publishers. Such books may be marketable in other countries. Possibly, film rights can be sold.

On the other hand, a local interest book, written by a first-time author, may sell just a few hundred copies. It may not even net any advance royalties if the publishing house concerned is a small one.

There is no easy way to fame and fortune as a writer. Yes, you can become successful, but, like most people, you must first expect to 'pay your dues' as the Americans say.

I'll give you some examples of people who have given up other work to concentrate full time on their writing, and are managing to make ends meet:

- Mary, a graduate of a university journalism programme, has given up her newspaper editing job to spend more time at home with her young son. She works as a 'stringer' for a city daily, covering news and features in the outlying area where she lives. She is also trying her hand at producing short stories which she will attempt to sell to women's magazines.

- Paul has had the plot of a novel going through his mind for some years. Now, having received a good severance package after being made redundant from his job, he's been given the impetus he needs. He will now attempt to make his book a reality.

- Recently retired at the age of 65, Henry is now free to pursue a lifelong dream of writing a book based on his hobby of collecting small antiques.

- Over the past twenty-five years, while earning her living as a local government officer, Martha has produced a number of do-it-yourself books which have enjoyed moderate success. By carefully investing her royalties she has reached the point where she can live modestly on the interest while branching out in other directions, such as fiction writing.

And of course there are those authors whose novels are so

popular that they net large sums of money from their books which regularly appear in the shops every year in time for Christmas. We won't refer to them as 'lucky' people because their success is well deserved. They, too, have 'paid their dues.'

Could you be a writer?

Now for a change of pace. Do you have what it takes to become a successful writer? Here's a quiz to help you decide. Tick the answer which most closely applies to you.

1   I want to be a writer because...
a   I love to write   ☐
b   I long for fame and fortune   ☐
c   My life story is fascinating and should be told   ☐

2   I work at my craft...
a   Every day   ☐
b   Once in a while   ☐
c   When inspiration strikes   ☐

3   When I complete a writing project I...
a   Rush with it to the post office   ☐
b   Review and revise   ☐
c   Put it away and start work on something else   ☐

4   When I receive a rejection I...
a   Tear up the manuscript   ☐
b   Produce a new copy and submit it elsewhere   ☐
c   I've never received one   ☐

5   I read...
a   Everything I can lay my hands on   ☐
b   Once in a while   ☐
c   Only on wet days   ☐

6   When an editor criticises my work I...
a   Phone up and vent my spleen   ☐
b   Write him off as a fool but keep my thoughts to myself   ☐
c   See if there is any merit in what he has to say   ☐

7   When I'm writing I allow myself to be
    interrupted by...
a   Phone calls and visitors   ☐
b   Household responsibilities   ☐
c   Nothing at all   ☐

8   When preparing to submit a manuscript I...
a   Think up a gimmick to get the editor's attention   ☐
b   Study the markets carefully   ☐
c   Think twice about sending it in case I'm turned down   ☐

9   Novels...
a   I know I could write one if only I could find the time   ☐
b   I will write a novel when I have time   ☐
c   I'm already writing a novel in secret   ☐

10 Learning new things...

a I learned everything I need to know when I was at
   school   ☐

b I want to learn all I can about the craft of writing   ☐

Now rate yourself as follows:

- 1 a-5, b-3, c-3
  When you have a compulsion to write, or you have a pressing reason for doing so, you have a good chance of success. Do be realistic, though; only the favoured few become millionaires by way of the pen. As for your fascinating life story: sorry, it is unlikely to become a best-seller.

- 2 a-5, b-3, c-3
  The professional writer spends long hours at the typewriter. The 'hobby' writer may achieve moderate success, but anyone who has to wait for inspiration to strike hasn't much chance. As with anything else in life, writing has to be worked at if you hope to get anywhere.

- 3 a-3, b-5, c-1
  Act in haste, repent at leisure. Polish your work before you send it out. Look at it with an objective eye. Is it something that you would like to read if you found it in a magazine? If the answer is no, by all means file it away. If it's good enough, send it out.

- 4 a-1, b-5, c-3
  One editor's meat is another editor's poison. Rejection is frustrating but it doesn't necessarily mean that your work is no good. If you've never received a rejection slip it probably means that you haven't sent out enough work. Nobody hits the target every time.

- 5 a-5, b-3, c-1

  The best way to learn to write is to read, read, read. Analyse other people's work. Why was it good enough to be published? Does it entertain, inform, fill a gap in the market?

- 6 a-0, b-3, c-5

  Editors usually know what is appropriate for their publications. If, on the other hand, you receive criticism which is patently unwarranted, turn your fury into productive avenues; continue to do the rounds of editors until you find someone who appreciates your work.

- 7 a-1, b-3, c-5

  There are times when we have to down tools to deal with a crisis. Minimise the number of interruptions by using an answering machine and letting it be known that you're unavailable during working hours.

- 8 a-0, b-5, c-3

  Gimmicks are the mark of an amateur and will exasperate, rather than intrigue an editor. Careful research of the market is more likely to impress. Nervous about sending out your work? You're in good company; most writers share your feelings. However, courage can make the difference between being published and unpublished.

- 9 a-1, b-3, c-5

  What makes published authors gnash their teeth? The person who accosts them at parties with the news that he, too, could write a book if he could only find the time. (The implication being that one doesn't need any special talent or training for the task). Serious writers just get on with the job.

- 10 a-1, b-5

  Nobody knows everything. The writer should always be open to new experiences. Styles change. The tastes of the reading public are constantly evolving. What worked twenty years ago may not be marketable today.

If you scored between 40 and 50, you're well on your way to becoming a writer. 25-39, you should learn the basics and get started. 24 or less: you may not have much luck as things stand, but we all have to start somewhere. If you make an effort to study the craft of writing who knows where it might lead?

Right now, you may not agree with our assessment of your chances. If, after working your way through this book, you're of the same opinion, take heart. The person who stubbornly insists, against all odds, that he is a writer, may well have what it takes to succeed.

The writing life

How much time should you devote to writing? That depends on what your goals are. The professional, who hopes to make a living from writing, must spend long hours in disciplined work. Anyone embarking on a novel should have the time to make a fairly sustained effort; you lose momentum by writing just a few pages once a month. The good news is that the novice, starting out in a small way by tackling the occasional short story or magazine article, can make this a spare-time activity.

Remember that there is more to writing than simply setting words down on paper. You must read as much as you possibly can. Discover what is being sold to newspapers and magazines these days. Take note of the books which are on the best seller lists. You don't necessarily want to jump on the same bandwagon but you should get a feel for what sells and what doesn't. Do you have an interest in collecting Victorian shoes? It's doubtful that many people would rush out to buy a book on the subject, but a magazine article is a good possibility if you approach it from an interesting angle.

Would you like to write a mystery novel? Read everything in that genre that you can find. Analyse the difference between the 'cosies' written in the 1930's and those being published today. Agatha Christie's books still have a tremendous following, as well they should, yet the demands of the reading public have changed. Modern novels written in the style of her early works would not find a publisher today.

You will find that much of your creative work will take place long before you sit down at the typewriter. There will be research to do and perhaps people to be interviewed. The story may well take shape in your head as you walk the dog or scrub the kitchen floor.

Published authors are often asked how long it takes them to write a book. They may hesitate before replying. Do they say six months, or three years, or whatever the actual typing time was, or do they consider the time it took for the theme to germinate in their minds?

Books often have their roots in lifelong experience. For example, the psychologist who produces a book about human relationships can only do so after following years of training and professional practice.

Tools of the trade

As a newcomer to the craft, what do you need in order to get started? The rock bottom basics are pen and paper, a good dictionary and a library card. However, you'll also need access to a typewriter, word processor or computer unless you can afford to pay someone to prepare manuscripts for you.

Some writers feel uncomfortable with modern technology and produce their early drafts in longhand. This is quite all right but the final draft is a different story; editors will expect to receive submissions in the form of neatly typed or printed out copy.

At the other end of the scale it's wonderful to have all the best modern aids under one roof, such as a computer, laser printer, photocopier, fax machine and a library full of useful reference books.

However, you certainly don't have to possess all these things in order to become a successful writer, and in fact the novice would be ill-advised to rush out and purchase expensive equipment before finding out if writing will become a means of earning a living or simply an enjoyable hobby.

If you are contemplating the purchase of a typewriter or word processor, ask yourself how long will it be before it pays for itself. While it may be some time before you actually receive payment for your work, there is another factor to be considered. If you plan to do a lot of writing - a 100,000 word novel, for instance - it may be cheaper in the long run to buy a word processor than to hire someone to do the typing.

The average charge today for having work prepared by a professional is £3 per 1000 words. If your novel doesn't sell you could be more than £300 out of pocket, whereas if you put that amount towards a word processor you'll be able to produce hundreds of manuscripts for the same outlay.

If you still prefer to hire an experienced typist, do ask what you'll receive for the basic fee and what counts as an 'extra'. Services vary widely because many professionals are individuals working out of their own homes.

- Some provide a draft copy for you to review before the final manuscript is prepared.

- Will you receive a duplicate copy, or just the original? (If a duplicate is an 'extra' take the original to have it photocopied. It may be less expensive that way).

- If a word processor or PC is used, what sort of printout will you receive? Laser is best; not all editors accept daisywheel printouts.

- Occasionally a diskette will be offered. If this involves an additional cost, it may not be worth your while. Editors initially require hard copy and even though some publishers like to produce books from an author's diskette, because this saves them money, the software used must be compatible with their own.

In the next chapter we discuss manuscript preparation.

2 YOU AND YOUR MANUSCRIPT?

- Presenting your work
- Preparing a CV
- The covering letter
- Keeping track
- The portfolio
- The scrapbook

When my mother answered the door one morning she found a representative of a religious sect standing on the doorstep. Too polite to send him on his way, she reluctantly listened to his patter. She later said that it all seemed to make sense - until he waved his hands to emphasize a point and she caught a glimpse of his grimy finger nails. 'Enough dirt under there to grow potatoes!' Turned off, she quickly closed the door in the man's face.

Don't provide editors with a reason for shutting the door on you. Your book or article could be prizewinning material, but that won't do you any good if it doesn't get a reading. A clean, beautifully produced typescript is more likely to be given a second look than an untidy piece of work which has numerous crossings-out.

Of course, there is no guarantee that such a well presented piece will result in a sale, but it will make that all-important good first impression. It is tempting for editors, swamped by unsolicited submissions, to throw out anything that looks amateurish. After all, if a writer can't be bothered to abide by the rules of manuscript preparation, what is to say that the article itself is correct in every detail? Research may have been sloppy or facts unchecked.

Presenting your work

So what are these rules? First of all, select unlined, white, A4 paper, and use only one side of the sheet.

Hand written work is not acceptable. While you may prefer to prepare your early drafts using a pen or pencil, the manuscript you mail out must be neatly typed.

If you use an ordinary typewriter, make sure that you use a new or nearly new ribbon. If you use a word processor or personal computer, see that the printout is easy to read. A laser printer is best, but expensive. Ink jets are acceptable, but unsuitable for book-length manuscripts because they take so long to print out. Some publishers state in directory listings that they are prepared to accept daisywheel printouts. Again, a dark ribbon is the order of the day.

Use a typeface that is plain and easy to read. The use of attention getting devices such as fancy fonts, or manuscripts peppered with italics and underlinings for emphasis, brand the writer as an amateur.

The writing must be double-spaced and unjustified type should be used. That is, the text should be flush with the left margin but ragged on the opposite side (e.g. not flush right). Use fairly wide margins. This leaves plenty of room, when you make a sale, for the editor to make changes to the piece and to insert directions for the typesetter.

Arrange your margins so that you have 25 lines to a page. This provides an editor with a rough idea at a glance of the length of your article at approximately 250 words per page. Of course, you will include a word count on your first page as well; round it off to the nearest 25 words. Example call 169 words 175.

Your spelling, grammar and punctuation should all be as good as possible. Yes, editors can, and do, tidy up any small slips, but they are not there to do the basic work for you. Apart from anything else, extensive editing costs money; editors have to be paid.

Spelling checkers on computer software are good up to a point. They will identify bloopers and typographical errors, as in 'the monkeey climbed the tree' but if you happen to mistakenly use a word which would be correct in another context, they won't pick it up. Compare these two sentences, which a spelling checker would pass as being correct:

- Not looking where I was going, I tripped over the cat.
- No looking where I was going, I tripped over the car.

Always read your manuscript carefully before you send it out.

Very few of us can get away with preparing only one draft of a book, story or article. In his autobiography, The Sport of Queens, author Dick Francis says that he is capable of producing just one draft of a novel, and that is that. Unfortunately, not everyone has his talent. For the rest of us, the order of the day is revise, revise, revise. You may only have one chance of impressing an editor. Don't blow it.

Each page should be numbered, and it's a good idea to put your name on every page as well, in case they get separated while being read. At the top of your first page, on the left-hand side, type your name, address, telephone number. Include the date and the word count.

Start a book manuscript on the next page. In the case of articles and short stories, drop several spaces and type the title in the middle of the page, starting your copy below. There is no need to agonize over finding the perfect title because that will probably be changed at the editing stage. Your working title is simply a device to identify your subject.

Most editors dislike staples. Use a paper clip to keep a small number of pages together. In the case of a book manuscript, put the loose pages in a suitably sized box or hold them together with a rubber band. Never put them in a folder or three-ring binder.

Articles and short stories should be mailed flat in a nine by twelve envelope, with your return address clearly marked on it.

Avoid gimmicks, such as coloured paper, fancy packaging or customised covers. Such attention-getting devices are amateurish and smack of desperation. The professional writer counts on good work and careful presentation to speak for him or her.

Your submission should be accompanied by a brief covering letter and your curriculum vitae, as well as clippings of previously published work or reviews of earlier books.

Your CV should include any information which will show

an editor that you are qualified to write an article or book. There are problems involved in taking on an unknown writer. Publishers need to be reassured that the work is correct in every detail. One hazard of the publishing business is that readers do not hesitate to point out errors; in fact they seem to do so with a certain amount of glee.

When Dick Francis began writing thrillers with a horse-racing background, publishers knew that his background material was true to life. Having been a top jockey, he was familiar with the racing scene. Perhaps you, too, have experience which you can use to your advantage.

Never, repeat, never, send off your only copy of that cherished manuscript. Packages can be lost or damaged in the mail. Occasionally, papers fall into a black hole at a publishing house and mysteriously disappear, or that manuscript, so lovingly prepared, comes home bearing coffee stains.

Before you mail out your book manuscript, (or more likely, sample chapters) make more than one set of photo copies of it. When the book is accepted you may be required to submit an additional copy to the publishing house for editing purposes.

In the case of a short story or article, make several copies. If the first submission is turned down, you always have a fresh copy ready to send out to the next editor.

Preparing a CV

In the workplace, there are two schools of thought on this

subject. You start by listing your first job and come up to the present day, or you work in reverse, beginning with your most recent occupation.

However, a standard CV may not impress an editor at all. Remember that you're not applying for a job; you're hoping to convince her that you're qualified to write the article or book in question.

You may wish to list educational qualifications, previously published work, and any experience relevant to the theme of your submission. You are not required to mention your age or marital status. Don't list your job history or hobbies, either, unless this information is connected with the manuscript you are trying to sell. For instance, you might have more luck in placing your article on survival rates of migratory birds if you mention your twenty year history of banding birds.

Don't be discouraged if you have nothing to put in a CV at this point. All you really need to become a published writer is to offer something that an editor wants to buy! In the absence of a CV, make the letter that accompanies your article work for you instead.

The Covering letter

The cover letter should be brief and to the point. Learn the name of the appropriate editor, (from the masthead of a recent issue of the magazine) and use it. Refrain from over-familiarity in your first approach. A straightforward letter might read as the example overleaf.

Barbara Mitford,
Bird Magazine,
20, Pigott Road,
Chester.
June 14, 1997.

Dear Ms. Mitford:
   Planting shrubs to attract birds
I enclose my 2500 word article on the
above subject for your consideration.
Over the past 40 years I have worked
as head gardener for Sir John Lovell,
an avid birdwatcher whose shrubs
attract thousands of seed-eating birds
every autumn. Your readers may be
interested to learn how even a small
garden can be adapted to attract birds
of all descriptions.
   I enclose a S.A.E. for your reply.
   I look forward to hearing from you.

   Yours truly,
   Frederick Parsloe

Keeping track

As soon as you feel ready to send out your first query or manuscript, there are three items that you should consider as essential equipment. They are: a submissions register, a portfolio and a scrapbook. By using these three aids on a regular basis you are guaranteed to become a more efficient and productive writer, gaining confidence as you go.

To set up a submissions register you need a three-ring binder divided into four sections:

- Submission records
- Positive responses
- Guidelines
- Useful rejections

Divide the submission sheets into five columns. In the first, record the title of the article or subject of the query you're sending out. In the next, the magazine or publishing house you're targeting. Then the date on which the package was sent out, followed by the date on which a reply is received. The last column records the type of response (assignment, go ahead on spec, no thanks).

Title	Magazine/ Publishing House	Date submitted	Date reply received	Response

It pays to have a number of queries or manuscripts in circulation at the same time. When one is turned down, immediately send it out again. A glance at the submission sheet tells you where the piece has already been sent.

After a while, a study of the submission sheet will provide you with other valuable information. Has an article on a certain topic gone out to numerous editors without success? Possibly you've been barking up the wrong tree with that particular subject.

The date columns are useful, too. How long has that piece been out there? Is it time to send a follow-up letter? What is the average turnaround time for each of the magazines you've selected? Can you afford to wait for six months or a year for a possible assignment, unable to submit that article elsewhere until the editor responds? Is it worth your while to submit other material to that publication if they are so slow? Which editors never respond at all, even when they have your SAE?

In sections two and three of the binder, file affirmative letters and magazine guidelines. Even when an outline has been approved it is important to bear in mind what the editor really wants and it's helpful to have his/her requirements in front of you as you work.

In section four, file the nice rejections (You can set fire to those impersonal, printed slips). What on earth is a nice rejection? When an editor takes the time to write a useful criticism, or says 'This won't do for us but why not send it to such and such a place' that letter is worth its weight in gold. It's good to know that somebody out there cares.

The portfolio

Writers of short pieces, including articles, stories and
poetry, really need to own a portfolio. The ideal is one of
those zippered, leather affairs with see-through, loose-leaf
pockets, but if expense is a consideration, an ordinary
school binder will do just as well. Here is what a portfolio
will do for you:

- It lets you assemble your work in one place, giving you a
  feeling of achievement as the book fills up.

- It helps you establish your own niche in the writing world by
  giving you a quick overview of what works for you. Compare
  your published articles with those that are unsuccessfully
  going the rounds from one slush pile to another.

- It provides a fast reference when you need to photocopy tear
  sheets of your published work to send to editors.

- A picture is worth a thousand words: a portfolio helps you
  make an impression when applying in person to write a
  newspaper columnist or company newsletter.

If you have no printed articles to put in your portfolio as
yet, take heart. Boost your confidence by inserting those
fillers or letters to the editor which have made it into print,
or manuscripts of your unpublished articles are good, too.
A body of work gathered in one place whispers the
message that you really are a writer, even if nobody else
recognises it - yet.

The scrapbook

There's nothing better than a personal scrapbook for boosting the writer's morale. You may be a novice now, but one of these days you'll have no trouble filling this treasury! Mine contains reviews of my published books, dreadful newspaper photos of myself, typed lists cataloguing appearances on television, the radio interviews done and the dinner meetings I've been invited to address.

There will be letters from readers in your scrapbook, too. I cherish the one from a woman who informed me that her family's Christmas dinner was late because she'd forgotten to put the turkey in the oven. She'd received one of my books for Christmas and become so absorbed in it that she lost track of time.

What will go into your first scrapbook? Perhaps the programme from the workshop you attended; the manuscript of the first story you read to your writers' circle; the night-school essay with the words Well Done! scrawled across the top. You'll be surprised at how quickly your scrapbook fills up. You'll know you've 'arrived' when you either have to resist the urge to save everything that comes along, or start a second volume.

Remember: even Shakespeare had to start somewhere. Use your three books as building blocks in your climb to success.

3 HOW & WHERE TO SUBMIT ? YOUR WORK

- Research your market
- Reference tools
- Query letters
- Submitting work
- Marketing your book

You have finished work on your article, story or book, revised and polished as best you can, and prepared a flawless manuscript. Now it's time to send it out. How do you go about it?

You must research the market before putting your manuscript in the envelope. One of the major causes of rejection is that writers target the wrong publication or publishing house when attempting to sell their work.

Research your market

Let's talk about articles and short stories first. If you've written a science fiction story it is useless to send it to Woman's Weekly, a magazine which publishes stories which are mainly in the romance genre. It is equally unproductive to send your story to a publication which only handles non-fiction.

All this should go without saying, but it's a fact of life that many novice writers fail to do the initial leg work which leads to success. Here's what you need to know:

- Before submitting work to any magazine, read several copies of the publication to get a grasp of house style. If you can't afford to purchase copies, try the public library.

- Write to the magazine asking for a copy of their writers' guidelines. Be sure to enclose a suitably sized stamped, self addressed envelope. Information in the guidelines usually includes the type of material which is bought from freelance writers, the required length for submissions, the usual rate of payment, and so on.

It may help if you address your submission to a specific editor by name. For example, if the fiction editor's name is Ann Harris, don't address the envelope to 'the editor' or to publisher Bridget Hawes. Editor's names are usually listed on the masthead of the magazine. Do check a recent issue of the publication when searching for this information in case Ann Harris has moved on. When all else fails, telephone the publication and ask for the fiction editor's name. Do not ask to speak to him or her directly!

Reference tools

- There are several excellent handbooks and directories on the market which list all the pertinent information on a majority of British publications. (Refer to the help list for more about these). Such books are valuable because they bring to your attention magazines which may be new to you, and they also spell out the particular material which these publications print.

These reference works come out annually, so it's important to look up the latest edition. In the publishing business there is a constant turnover of staff, and magazines do tend to come and go.

There are several excellent magazines for writers which will be listed in the help list section of this book. Their market information is often more up-to-date than what is offered in the handbooks because the magazines are printed monthly.

Query letters

While short stories are usually submitted in their entirety you may find that, where non-fiction is concerned, sending a query letter will work better for you. This can save you considerable time, money and frustration.

However good your idea is and no matter how well researched and written your article might be, there are a number of reasons why it could be turned down. The magazine might be overstocked with freelance submissions; perhaps they ran a similar story in a recent issue, or currently have one in the pipeline. Perhaps certain sections of the publication are dealt with in-house and not open to the freelance writer.

The first paragraph of your query letter should attract the editor's attention, pique her curiosity. You must explain what you mean to do, point out why it would appeal to readers, mention the probable length of the piece and reassure her that you are capable of following through on your idea. Overleaf is one (purely fictional) example.

John Dean,
Quirks of History,
5, London Lane,
Manchester .

Dear Mr. Dean:
You can imagine how excited I
was to learn that an ancestor of
mine was William Shakespeare's
mistress. Family documents that
have recently come into my
possession bear this out and it
appears that she may have
collaborated with him in writing
some of his comedies !

I'll tell the story of
Shakespeare and Mistress Margery
Culpeper in a 2,000 word article
which is sure to appeal to
scholars the world over. There
is some evidence that when their
relationship ended he presented
Margery with a copy of an
unpublished play which so far
has remained undiscovered. I'm
prepared to let you examine the
documents to prove that this is
not a hoax.

I enclose some clippings of work
previously published in history
magazines.
Yours truly, Peter Winterbotham,
MA.

Submitting work

The practise of making multiple submissions of complete manuscripts is frowned on in the trade, but you may certainly send query letters to more than one publication at a time.

I once purchased two different magazines at the same time, only to find that the same short story had appeared in each. As a paying customer I felt cheated; the editors must have been gnashing their teeth. The rule of submission is: one at a time.

You must include a self-addressed envelope, stamped with sufficient postage, in order to have your submission returned. The cost of postage being what it is, I usually enclose a business-sized envelope, stating in my covering letter that unwanted manuscripts can be destroyed. I work on computer and it is easy to print out a new, clean, copy to send to the next editor on my list.

Once your manuscript is in the mail, you must sit back and wait. It is not acceptable to ring up the editor after a few days to ask what is going on. Sometimes you will receive an acknowledgement saying that your submission has been received, sometimes not. Some writers like to enclose a stamped, self addressed postcard for this purpose.

You will usually receive a reply within a month or two, but very occasionally the weeks will go by without any response. After a reasonable period you may then wish to send a follow-up letter, asking for an explanation.

This calls for some decision-making on your part. An

exasperated editor may reject your piece if he feels hassled; if he has been holding it in the hope of using it in the future it would be too bad if hasty interference spoiled your chances.

How long is too long? You'll have to go with your gut feeling on this one. A few days after submitting a query to a certain magazine I received an enthusiastic phone call from the editor, asking me to produce the article. The piece was duly submitted. Three months went during which I heard nothing. I then wrote a polite letter asking about the status of the article, explaining that it was not a multiple submission and I hoped to place it elsewhere if she had no use for it. Again, there was no response.

At the six month mark I wrote again, formally withdrawing my article and stating that I intended to send it elsewhere. It went off to another magazine, was accepted, and appeared in print a few weeks later.

Marketing your book

The strategy for marketing a book is rather different from the methods outlined for articles and short stories. Here again a writer's handbook is an invaluable tool because submission requirements vary from one publishing house to another. You can avoid disappointment by a careful reading of the entries. Information given may include:

- The type of books published by a particular company, eg romance novels, environmental studies, text books, local histories. We cannot stress too often that it only leads to disappointment when writers send their manuscripts to houses which do not publish in that genre.

- Whether they will look at unsolicited manuscripts. Companies who refuse to consider unsolicited or unagented material will return it unread.

- How submissions should be made. Some houses like to see a complete manuscript; most prefer three sample chapters and an outline or synopsis. If, after the editor has read this sample, she feels that the work shows promise, you will be invited to submit the rest.

You sometimes hear about books being accepted on an outline or proposal alone. Will this happen to you? When it comes to fiction, it's unlikely that the novice author will be given a contract before a book has actually been written. Once your first book has been accepted you could possibly be contracted to write more, especially if your story has series potential. The most likely scenario is that a clause in your initial contract will stipulate that your publisher be given first refusal on your next book.

By contrast, a non-fiction book will sometimes be commissioned on an outline and sample chapters alone. Any approach to a publisher should be accompanied by a curriculum vitae which supports your claim to being qualified to write this book.

A publisher is more likely to show an interest in your proposal if you are an expert in your field, are well known to the public, or if the subject matter appears to be commercially viable.

4 DEALING WITH REJECTION ?

- Don't take it personally
- Reasons for rejections
- Minimising the sting
- What they say and what they mean

Nobody likes rejection. Unfortunately, it is part of the business of writing and we all have to learn to deal with it. It helps to know that in having our work turned down we are in the best of company.

Indubitably, Catherine Cookson was born to write, yet when she first submitted a story, hoping it would help her gain entrance to a creative writing course she received a curt note from the instructor: 'Advise this author not to take up writing as a career.' Today, millions of her novels are in print and they have been translated into many different languages.

Author John Creasey reportedly received 753 rejection slips before his career took hold. In time, he published more than 500 novels.

American author Mary Higgins Clark, whose suspense novels also sell millions of copies, received forty rejection slips over a six year period before her first short story sold.

The list of writers who have triumphed over initial setbacks is endless. The message here is not that the new writer stands to be rebuffed if he dares to submit his work to those all-powerful editors, but that perseverance pays. Never give up!

Don't take it personally

Of course, this admonition always comes from established writers, who are able to look back on their early struggles with equanimity. It's not so easy to maintain a positive outlook when nobody seems to appreciate your work.

How will you deal with rejection? To begin with, you mustn't take it personally. This is easier said than done; the true writer is seldom a thick-skinned person. In order to realise our full creative potential we leave ourselves open to emotions and new experiences and this makes us unusually vulnerable to 'the slings and arrows of outrageous fortune' (even Shakespeare probably had his share of rejections).

Reasons for rejection

There may be many reasons why your work, sent out with such high hopes, finds its way back to you. Some possibilities are:

- The magazine or publishing house may have already purchased a similar work from someone else.

- Editors may have planned future issues around a theme, and your piece doesn't fit in.

- They may have a backlog of suitable articles or stories and be unable to take on anything more at present.

- Your piece could be excellent, yet still not match the editor's concept of what works in the scheme of things.

- The time may not be right for this particular piece to be published. Like everything else, the fashion in writing styles does come and go. Some years ago, short stories had to end with a 'twist'. Later, this trend was considered old hat. Today, stories with a surprise ending are once again becoming popular.

- Many publishing houses will not read unsolicited manuscripts and will return them unread - and only if you have enclosed sufficient postage.

On the other hand, is it possible that the fault could be yours? Ask yourself these questions:

- Did I target the right sort of magazine or publishing house? As any editor will tell you, they frequently receive submissions that are hopelessly wrong for their needs. While working as an editor for a company which published regional history books I received manuscripts of novels, autobiographies and even poetry, even though our listing in the various directories clearly stated our requirements.

- Was my manuscript properly prepared, and accompanied by a short, clear letter? (Refer to the chapter on manuscript preparation).

- Could my work have been improved?

Minimising the sting

How do you feel when that nasty brown envelope lands on your door mat? It's okay to feel angry, particularly when you know in your bones that this is a fine piece of work. Try to fight back the urge to give the editor a piece of your mind. The publishing community is a small one and difficult authors soon make a name for themselves among editors.

Let your anger work for you. Keep sending out that piece. Keep on writing. Be determined to prove those rejecting editors wrong. Think about the 'expert' who rudely rejected Catherine Cookson. She managed to rise above the pain to become one of the world's best-loved writers. Can you imagine a better way to get your own back?

There are ways in which you can minimise the sting of rejection.

- Before a manuscript goes out for the first time, compile a list of several suitable places where you might send it. As soon as a rejected article reaches home, mail it out again. Don't give yourself time to brood.

- Always have more than one piece in circulation at the same time. Then, if one comes back, you won't feel too badly because you'll still have hope for the others.

But what if you're a would-be novelist? Wouldn't it be a waste of time to keep churning out books without definite publication in view? In this case, diversify. While attempting to sell your first novel get started on the second, and meanwhile, write some other things, such as short stories or magazine articles.

By keeping a constant flow of material in circulation, you'll be keeping hope alive, you'll be perfecting your craft and you'll eventually discover your right metier. If you can't sell work in one field, you may be successful in another.

Another way to cope with disappointment is to set up what I call a 'Wednesday Box'. This is a small container in which you file slips of paper inscribed with messages to yourself. For example: 'book turned down', or 'computer glitch destroyed 20,000 words' or 'editor totally unreasonable!' You get the idea.

Once the slips are in the box, forget about the episodes that prompted you to write them until the following Wednesday, when you take them out and read them. A week can make a great deal of difference. Surprisingly, most of the crises seem to pass before the week is up and even with those that still loom large it becomes obvious that life has gone on. In other words, this little box helps to put things in perspective.

Another alternative is to pamper yourself with some inexpensive and non-fattening treat. Consider walking beside a rushing river, taking a new book out of the library, or renting a good video. You deserve the best!

What they say and what they mean

Now a word about the rejection slips themselves. They come in different shapes and sizes. These include:

- A printed card which explains that 'your submission does not meet our requirements at this time.' Chattier variations will explain that 'due to the volume of submissions we receive we are unable to make individual comments.' Computer wizardry makes it possible to include your name at the top, making the rejection seem less impersonal.

- Occasionally a form letter goes out, saying essentially the same thing, but adding 'Good luck in placing your work.' (Too bad that one can't gauge the tone of voice from a letter; are they sincere or does this really mean that you have a better chance of winning the Irish Sweepstakes?)

This sort of thing gives rise to all sorts of questions, such as why didn't it meet their requirements? If you have carefully studied their guidelines and read copies of their magazine or studied books published by their publishing house, then you are left with the conclusion that what you offered isn't what they need at this time. This does not mean that your submission falls short of the required standard. Send if off to the next name on your list.

- A few magazines actually use a check list of possible reasons why they have to turn down your work. 'We are overstocked at present' or 'your piece was too slight for publication.'

Such lists are useful to the beginning writer, once the first flush of indignation passes, so why don't more firms use them?

- You know that your chances are improving when you receive a small, hand written note which says something like 'I enjoyed reading your article, but unfortunately it isn't quite what we need for Caterpillar Magazine.' Cherish this one. You must be getting closer to your goal; a flesh and blood editor has responded to your submission! Contrary to what you might have been thinking, you haven't been tossing your work into a void.

- If you ever receive a letter of friendly criticism from an editor, telling you that your story is a 'near miss', paste it in your scrapbook and never let it go. These are few and far between because editors are extremely busy people who receive hundreds of manuscripts each week. If one takes the time to write to you in this fashion, you'll know she means what she says. Editors just don't hand out encouragement to people unless they mean it; most are kindly souls who shrink from offering false hope.

Rejection is painful, but do not give up. Even if they are never published, every article, story or book that you write is a stepping stone to success because you are perfecting your craft as you go along. Some day you'll receive that beautiful acceptance letter, and an even more welcome cheque, and then all the hard work will seem worthwhile.

A woman who has gone through the discomforts of pregnancy, culminating in labour pains, will tell you that none of that seems to matter once she has held her baby in her arms. As both a mother and an author, I know from happy experience that it can be the same for the writer who achieves publication at last.

5 NON-FICTION WRITING

- Approach
- Breaking in
- Finding ideas
- Magazine writing
- Books
- Selling your book
- Copyright and plagiarism

One of the characters in *Alice's Adventures in Wonderland* has a piece of advice that many novice writers take to heart. 'Begin at the beginning,' the king said gravely, 'and go on until you come to the end.'

While it may be excellent advice for some, there is no 'right way' to produce written work. Of course, if you hope to sell that work you will have to keep to certain rules, such as length, style and correct English, but the route taken to arrive at that finished product will be solely up to you.

Approach

Do you remember those English lessons at school, where, before starting on an essay you were required to produce an outline, paragraph by paragraph, beginning with an introduction and following through to a logical conclusion?

Not everyone can work in that way. You may begin with a

certain idea only to find the story taking off in an unforeseen direction when you uncover unsuspected material while during research, or hoped for information proves impossible to find. I learned this early in life. After earning low marks in class I hit on a wonderful idea: write the essay first and do the outline later!

Some people choose to write the conclusion of an article first. Some authors of non-fiction books produce the easy chapters first, saving the difficult bits until the end. Computer technology has considerably lightened the load for people who work best in this slightly disorganized manner; paragraphs or whole pages can be moved about without you having to retype whole slabs of text.

Yet, even though it's fine for you to compose in the way which you find most comfortable, your old teacher's advice should not be entirely disregarded. An outline works well for many people.

- It provides you with a starting point by helping you to marshal your ideas.

- You can see at a glance if there is enough meat in the idea to make the piece worthwhile.

- When seeking an assignment you must be able to provide an editor with some idea of the direction your article is taking. She can't assign work blindfolded.

And speaking of assignments: when it comes to articles and news stories you'll find yourself working under one of three conditions.

If a piece is assigned to you (as a result of your query, or because an editor has approached you, the expert) it means that in all probability it will be used and paid for, if you meet all the required criteria (deadline, length, acceptable standard).

In this case find out if they pay a 'kill fee', a portion of the agreed payment, if the piece is an accepted piece, but never used after all.

You may be asked to write 'on speculation' if the editor likes your basic idea but can't make a firm decision before seeing the completed piece. Novices are often asked to write on spec if there is doubt in the editor's mind that they can follow through.

Material received 'over the transom' refers to unsolicited work.

Breaking in

It's advisable for the novice to test the waters by starting in a small way. Consider writing letters to the editor, submitting work to your parish magazine, sending press releases to your local newspaper. This is good practice for you and acts as a confidence builder if this material appears in print. A number of women's magazines pay £10 or £15 for any letter they print, not bad for a few lines of writing.

- Don't put all your eggs in one basket. Try a variety of endeavours.

- Offer to write a column for your local weekly newspaper. Decide what your theme is to be, then prepare two or three samples to take with you when you approach the editor.

- Find out which magazines accept short filler material or humorous true stories. *Reader's Digest* is one of the top markets for this; they have specific requirements so read the magazine to see what these are.

Isn't there tremendous competition here? Certainly, but they do use dozens of pieces each month and one of them could be yours.

Finding ideas

Established writers are often asked where they find their ideas. Well, ideas are *easy* enough to come by; the trick is to convert them into interesting, polished pieces of work which editors will snap up.

Let's say that you hope to produce a column, or some feature articles, for your local newspaper. Your interest is local history, so you prepare one or two pieces, no more than 1000 words in length, and beard the editor in his den. Fifteen minutes later, after a heady discussion of (as usual) the length each article should be, deadlines and the rate of pay, you find yourself outside the office, filled with excitement. Where do you go next?

- Visit the senior citizens' home. Residents can give first-hand accounts of local happenings in years gone by. Did anyone there work as a gamekeeper, a housemaid, a groom in the stables of a stately home long ago?

- Consult local history books. You cannot use the author's copyrighted work but it may spark ideas of your own.

- Back issues of the local newspaper will help you to verify facts.

- Was a famous person born in your community? Can you come up with inside information which will let you tell her story from a hitherto unexplored angle?

Magazine writing

You can approach magazine writing in one of two ways. You can study the magazines that appeal to you and try to come up with a fresh idea that seems to fit into their scheme of things, or you can develop an idea from scratch before seeking publications whose editors may be interested.

Now, let's say you've always been interested in how bees make honey. What are the prospects here? There are not likely to be any takers if you produce a factual essay on the life cycle of the honey bee. If there were, you can be sure that some expert bee keeper has already beaten you to it. So, you need another angle.

Look at these suggestions and try to decide where you might attempt to place the following stories:

- Your neighbour's daughter is allergic to bee stings. She was recently involved in a dramatic incident where her life was saved through the prompt action of the local postman. Interview the hero, the girl or the mother (or all three) for an 'as told to' piece. A side-bar could include information on why some people are allergic to bee stings, and how many people die in Britain each year as a result. Where do you find such information and how can you ascertain that it is accurate and up-to-date?

- The local vicar keeps bees. He likes to mention them in his sermons, drawing parallels with Biblical stories. Parishioners chuckle about the time his bees swarmed when he was about to perform a wedding ceremony. There may be a human interest story there.

- Mrs Cora Dodson, 90, remembers the days when her mother 'told the bees' about important happenings in the family. This leads into a discussion of other country lore of the turn of the century.

What are editors looking for? Subjects which are suited to their particular publication, a fresh approach, a well written article that begins by catching their attention and keeps up the momentum until the end. Remember: if an article fails to interest an editor it might well leave readers cold, and readers expect to be informed and entertained.

Here are two possible lead-ins to Mrs Dodson's story. Which of the two would be more likely to encourage you to read on?

- A   Mrs Cora Dodson, 90, is a resident at the Journey's End Retirement Home. She seldom has visitors so whenever she has a captive audience she likes to talk about the past...

- B   When Father fell off his bicycle, his wife rushed to the hive at the bottom of the garden and told the bees about the mishap. Now aged 90, Mrs Cora Dodson remembers the incident as well as if it happened yesterday...

Now write a suitable lead paragraph of your own. You can surely do better than the foregoing examples but remember, this is not science fiction! When writing for public consumption, you must get your facts straight. The consequences of failing to do so can be serious, ranging from embarrassing the publisher to causing difficulty if readers come to grief by acting on something you've said.

Books

It seems there are as many topics for possible non-fiction books as there are stars in the sky, and you are certain that you've thought up a good one. Will it be your own life story? A biography of the person who created Rupert Bear? A guide to collecting antique glass, a subject on which you are an expert? Something about exploring West Wales by bicycle? The story of your local railway?

Writing your own memoirs is seldom a paying proposition. Recording the details of your life story for family consumption may be greatly appreciated by your children but outsiders will not shell out good money to read about them unless of course you happen to be Princess Diana.

Don't be put off, though; instead of seeking publication write about your childhood for your own amusement. It may bring you great pleasure while you are learning the craft of writing. Continual practice can only improve any storytelling talent that you possess.

The other ideas are all good, but before proceeding go to a large library and look through the catalogue index to see such books have not been done before. If they have, there may not be a market for new versions of the same.

Try to get ahead of the crowd. There is a current fashion

for books about angels but if you begin research on another one today, chances are the fad will have passed by the time your book comes into print, three or four years down the road. On the other hand, a topic which is too esoteric may have limited appeal.

Selling your book

Here again there are two methods of approach. You can complete the book and start making the rounds of suitable publishers, or you can approach a publisher with an idea to ask if he will commission the book. The latter approach is more likely to be successful if you are an established writer, an expert in your field or if you have the inside track on some hot topic.

Do research the market carefully and avoid submitting manuscripts to companies who don't handle work in your genre, or who state that unsolicited material is always returned unread.

Whether you have completed a book or merely have a proposal to submit, begin the road to publication by making up a promotional package to send out. This will include:

- A brief cover letter.
- The working title of the book with copy prepared as a jacket blurb. The publisher will not necessarily use either your title or the accompanying blurb if the book is accepted. At this stage the intent is to 'sell' the concept to her.
- Your curriculum vitae as it applies to your writing life. Knowing

that you work as a waiter and collect bugs in your spare time will not help your cause, unless your subject is collecting bugs as a hobby.

- It may help your cause if you have worked as a newspaper reporter, or have long years of experience in your field of expertise, or if your articles have been previously published in magazines. However, there is no law that forces you to confess that you are a novice writer.

- Sample chapters of the book, preferably the first three.

- Include a list of chapter headings, giving the main points in each. Editors will understand that these details are likely to alter as the book takes shape. That said, a work which differs widely from the original concept is hardly likely to find favour with the people who gave you a tentative acceptance.

- Explain what you think the market potential might be. A publisher will want to have a grasp of whether this book is a good investment. Could it be used as a school text book? Have you a list of 101 nature lovers' groups whose members would love to buy your treatise on water fowl?

- Have you any ideas on promotion for the book?

Copyright and plagiarism

Before getting started, you should understand what is meant by plagiarism and copyright. Plagiarism is the use of someone else's work while claiming it as your own.

Copyright means you own the rights to work which you have created and have the sole right to assign its use to other people, such as publishers. For more information on assigning rights, please refer to chapter 8: Earnings, Tax and Contracts.

As a young reporter on a weekly newspaper I was approached by a schoolgirl who hoped to write a column about potted plants. She had samples to show and it soon became clear that the girl had simply extracted basic information from an encyclopedia, rearranging the sentences here and there.

When complained to, the editor insisted that the girl should not be told the reason for the rejection, because her feelings would be hurt. I felt that it would have been better in the long run if someone had gently given the child the facts of (writing) life.

The laws of copyright, and the rules covering plagiarism, are strict and yet many people either seem to be unaware of them or choose to ignore them.

I recently received a letter from a woman who asked if I could send her a copy of one of my books (a local history now out of print) 'As I want to use some of it in my family history book and it would be a nuisance to have to photocopy so many pages.' This took my breath away because using slabs of someone else's work is illegal, and so is photocopying pages of someone else's printed work.

Breach of these laws constitutes theft, and the unwary user can be punished accordingly. As soon as your work is committed to print, even before it is published, you own the copyright. Traditionally this protection has extended to fifty years after the death of the author, but at the time of writing these laws have recently been changed and the time span will now be extended to 70 years. Should your work be published outside Britain, be aware that copyright law differs in many other countries. A further point: ideas and facts cannot be copyrighted. It is your way of writing about them which is unique.

Non-fiction writers are often required to provide illustrations to supplement their work and the availability of maps and pictures often helps to sell an article to an editor. Be aware that photographs and drawings are also the intellectual property of their creators.

There is an exception to the rule: you do not own the copyright of material produced while working for an employer. Photographs you may have taken while on the staff of a newspaper belong to the publisher, and, should you later wish to use them in a book featuring your work, you will have to obtain his written permission.

6 CRAFTING FICTION

- The challenge
- The genres
- Rules of the game
- Beyond the basics
- Questions of length

Fiction is perhaps the most interesting and creative form of writing from the author's point of view. Characters seem to spring from nowhere, and many authors say that the development of these fictional people is almost as much of a surprise to their creators as it is to the reader. They seem to take on a life of their own within the confines of the plot.

The challenge

On the down side, fiction, particularly the novel, is challenging to write and difficult to sell. Book publishers receive hundreds of submissions each month yet publish only a fraction of that number.

Placing a novel can be an uphill battle, but it certainly isn't impossible. My own first novel sold to the first publisher it was submitted to; why shouldn't you be just as lucky? Of course, luck plays only a small part in the submission game; I'd carefully researched the market before posting off the manuscript.

Markets for certain types of short story have dwindled in recent years as economic down-sizing takes its toll, yet every week a number do appear in British magazines.

Yes, the competition is strong, but should you let this factor put you off writing? Not at all. Hard work and persistence will certainly be the order of the day, but it almost always pays off in the end.

Do remember that the actual writing is only one aspect of the craft. Here are some points for you to consider:

- Publishers may be swamped with manuscripts, but many of those submissions will be turned down because their authors failed to follow the rules. Perhaps a gardening book was sent to a fiction house, or the manuscript was too long or too short for the genre.

- Competition may well be fierce but hundreds of books are published every year. Your novel could be among them.

- Many of the world's best-loved authors are not getting any younger and will one day, alas, decide to retire. Some of today's novices will, by that time, be ready to step into their shoes.

- Writers whose books head the best seller lists today, or whose stories appear regularly in top magazines, all had to 'pay their dues.' In most cases they first met with rejection. In others, they had several books published before becoming a household name.

Rosamunde Pilcher's book, *The Shell Seekers*, is tremendously popular around the world and has been

filmed and recorded on audiotape, yet this was no
overnight success story. Before that book came out she
had amassed a respectable body of work, with many short
stories and published books to her credit.

Other leading authors have had similar experiences.
Although their first major success may have come from
being in the right place at the right time, they all have three
things in common: the will to write, belief in their abilities,
and a determination not to give up.

When you have completed your first short story or novel,
and sent it off to a suitable editor, sit down and start on the
next. Keep the pot boiling. There are two things to
remember here:

- If you always have several things in circulation at once, it
  won't hurt as much if one is turned down; you will still have
  hope for the others. Re-submit as soon as you can.

- Possibly your first effort really isn't worthy of publication,
  but the next one may be. All writers learn by doing. Think of
  it as a stepping stone on the road to success.

The genres

Fashions come and go and it is important to keep abreast
of the trends. The books of Charles Dickens are
acknowledged classics. Several have been filmed over the
years and Oliver Twist was the basis for the musical,
Oliver. Doesn't this sound like every writer's dream come
true?

The question is, if an author selected similar subject matter today, writing in that ponderous Victorian style and dwelling heavily on Britain's social problems, would you buy his book to read on the train?

Today's book buying public has different tastes: a faster pace, less description and more dialogue, and a more upbeat approach, at least at the end of the book. They also want more variety, which is good news for the author.

Books on the market today include: literary novels, romance, historicals, suspense, mystery, horror, science fiction, erotica and crime. Writing for children is an exciting field, ranging everything from the small, heavily illustrated book to tales of horror for young adults.

Short stories are also needed in most of these categories. A few genres have whole magazines devoted to them. For example, stories by a number of British writers appear regularly in two American publications, *Ellery Queen's Mystery Magazine* and the *Alfred Hitchcock Mystery Magazine*.

Needless to say, each type of fiction has its own requirements regarding length and style.

Rules of the game

Although you can give your characters free rein and nobody can tell you that a certain episode 'didn't happen like that' as they might in non-fiction, there are rules to be followed. There must be a plot, and everything in the story must have its logical place. There is no point in introducing a mysterious stranger in chapter three if he never appears again or has no effect on the story line.

Both the short story and the full-length book must start out with a hook, that is, something to pique the reader's curiosity and make her want to read on. There must also be an effective ending, or the reader will feel cheated.

Books in a series, where events change but similar characters appear, should be complete in themselves. The reader should care enough about the protagonist to want to buy the sequel, but it's unfair to end the book with a cliffhanger situation. In the silent movie days, when the villain tied the heroine to the railway track and left her there until the following week, patrons flocked to the cinema to see what would happen next. People of the 1990's have more options. When a book fails to appeal it may not be read through to the end, and they may not buy that author's work again.

Unless a book is particularly gripping, it won't be read at one gulp. The logical place to stop reading is at the end of a chapter so, ideally, this is the place to provide the reader with something that makes him want to keep turning the pages.

Note that there is a difference between literary fiction and books in other genres. In the latter, twists and turns in the plot make the story interesting. Literary fiction portrays real life situations and the story moves more slowly. Top notch prose, coupled with an understanding of human nature and what makes people act as they do, must compensate for the lack of high drama in the story line.

When we speak of 'real life situations' we mean the sort of

believable, everyday matters that could happen to any of us, occurrences with which we can identify.

A story based on real life does not necessarily mean something which really took place. As an editor, I often received letters which began something like this. 'My grandmother had a really hard/interesting/ successful life, and I wish to tell her story.'

Of course you love Grandma, but the problem is that her life story has no plot. Even if you fictionalise it, your knowledge of the real woman may stand in the way of your developing her character to the point where readers will identify with her. And can you really *see* yourself describing her love life in detail?

In most genres, conflict must form part of the plot. If the reader doesn't care about the characters and their ultimate fate, he won't finish the book. Compare these two women:

- Case one   Grace, an unmarried secretary, feels she can no longer go on living. A nasty new colleague has walked into the job promotion that Grace has been hoping for, and snapped up the handsome boss, to boot. The next ten chapters consist of a flashback to the unhappy years prior to this point, as Grace asks herself 'Why does this always happen to me?'

- Case two   Solange, a successful plastic surgeon, has been receiving death threats. On several occasions she has been followed home by an unknown man in a blue Volvo. Is she the victim of a psychopath, or could this have something to do with Franklin, her estranged husband?

No editor will consider buying the saga of poor, neurotic

Grace. It will do the author no good to say 'Ah, but the story heats up in chapter eleven. Grace throws caution to the winds, goes on holiday to Italy, meets a childless millionaire and has a torrid affair which ends when he dies of a heart attack, having willed all his money to her.'

People buy books to be entertained. They do not expect to wade through ten chapters of gloom and doom before they can lose themselves in the tale.

Solange's story holds more promise. Who is stalking her, and why? What will happen to her? We know that she will probably escape with her life and that the book will have a happy ending, with a marriage proposal from the police detective who has handled her case, but we want to see what happens to her along the way.

This brings us to another point. A popular caution for fiction writers these days is 'Write what you know.' Does this always hold true? Sometimes it does. If you are a plastic surgeon by profession, or a hospital nurse, you already have the ideal background in which to place Solange.

American author Andrew Greeley writes suspense novels featuring clergy and people who are members of the Roman Catholic Church. As a Catholic priest Greeley has no need to research the background for these books, he has this material at his fingertips. He knows the mind set of his characters and how they are likely to react in given situations.

On the other hand, British author Ellis Peters has never been a nun, yet that wonderful medieval monk, Brother Cadfael, is utterly believable, the result of superb research on her part. Surely Brother Cadfael really existed. . .

So, then, the choice is yours. You can write about the Solanges of this world without ever having performed a face lift, but do make sure that your research has a practical aspect to it. Could you obtain permission to visit an operating room when it is not being used? Soak up the atmosphere: the smell of disinfectant, the glare of the overhead lights. Where does the surgeon scrub up? Where does he keep his ordinary clothes when he changes into operating room greens? Where is the patient taken before she comes out of the anaesthetic?

Where would Solange have given patients their first consultation? Does she subscribe to the modern computer technology that provides 'before and after' views of the patient's face? Does she in fact perform cosmetic surgery at all, or does she work instead with accident victims? Such information will flesh out the book and make it more interesting; most readers like to learn something new. Even when the book is meant as light entertainment it is important to get the facts straight. One slip of the scalpel and you're likely to hear from half a dozen irate surgeons.

Beyond the basics

There are a number of excellent books on the market which deal with the various aspects of fiction writing. These provide valuable insight into the craft. While you may well have the gift of story telling there is always something new to be learned. Why find your way through trial and error when such good reference works are available to you? Would you take a walking tour of a strange country without at least taking along a map?

Writing magazines are also handy because they contain articles which zero in on special aspects of creative writing, such as dialogue and point of view.

Questions of length

- Q   I've just completed a 30,000 word western novel. Can you name any publishers who might be interested?

  A   I'm sorry to say that you are unlikely to find a publisher for such a short manuscript. Your book would have to be double that size to even be considered. As for publishers, visit the library and look for books of this type. Estimate the number of words in the book and take note of who their publishers are. Consult one of the writing directories to see if these houses are still publishing in this genre and, if so, whether they will accept unsolicited manuscripts.
  The publishing industry is constantly changing. Publishing houses merge, go out of business or change direction. Editors come and go. The only way to keep abreast of these changes is to consult an up-to-date directory. If in doubt, phone the publishing house and ask the receptionist what their current policy is.

- Q   I have some ideas for writing short stories. Does length matter?

  A   It does if you hope to see them in print. Stories can range from 'short-shorts' (generally between 600 and 1000 words) to several thousand. Few are more than 3,500 words long.
  What sort of stories do you have in mind? Light romance?

Mystery? Literary? When you compose a story without first considering the market, this is rather like putting the cart before the horse. Know what you want to write, then investigate the publications which handle that sort of thing. (Here again, follow the library/directory route). Read the magazines for which you hope to write. Send away for their writer's guidelines, enclosing a SAE for their reply.

How many words do they ask for? Stay within that range. Believe it when we say that editors know what is best for their publications. If they want science fiction don't send them a literary short story hoping that they may change their minds when they see how good it is.

● Q   I've noticed that the books in my local shop come in all shapes and sizes. Is there a general rule of thumb I can follow when starting my novel?

A   Publishers do have specific requirements. Spy thrillers usually run to 70,000 words or so. Mainstream novels can range from 70,000 to 90,000 words. Blockbusters run between 100,000 and 150,000. Harlequin romances average 55,000 words with variations in their other lines.

7 TEAMWORK: THE EDITOR, THE AGENT & YOU ?

- Editors
- Editors' expectations
- You have rights too!
- Agents
- Finding an agent
- Agents' charges

A writer was under contract to us for a second book. Sales of her first had not lived up to expectations but the publisher hoped to recoup his investment from the new work, which had more promising subject matter. This is why contracts often specify that the publisher has first refusal on a subsequent work; it is expensive in terms of time and money to shepherd a new author through the various stages of the publishing process and to promote his book. In theory, all this is easier the second time around.

When our author learned that a copy of her manuscript was about to be sent to an Arts Council where, we hoped, we would receive a publishing grant, she balked, afraid that her precious work would be stolen and published under someone else's name.

The end result was disappointment on both sides. The author was released from her contract and to this day her book has not been published. Presumably a similar scenario was played out when she tried to place it elsewhere.

Surprisingly, many novice writers are afraid their work will be stolen by unscrupulous editors. This is nonsense. Any professional who attempted such a ploy would very soon be in trouble, without a job and on the wrong end of a lawsuit. Nor would they need to attempt such a thing; publishers have their pick of more manuscripts than they know what to do with.

Editors

In general, editors are a hard-working breed who play a vital role in the publishing chain. A good one is worth her weight in gold. There are, of course, less efficient ones to be found; editors are only human, but quite often any misunderstandings stem from a lack of knowledge on the writer's part as to what really happens in the publishing world.

The writer's first contact with an editor is usually when he submits his manuscript for consideration. All being well, the editor sends back a letter of acceptance and, in due course, the author sees his work in print.

Before this happens, however, a great deal goes on behind the scenes that the writer knows little about. At a 'small' magazine or small press, operated by one or two people, the submission may be read by the publisher himself, or scrutinized by a freelance editor who works for the company.

In a larger firm it will pass through several hands, often beginning with an assistant. The editor who feels that the manuscript has potential may not have the final say in the matter but simply passes it on to the next level with a recommendation.

This is particularly true of the book manuscript; several people may read it before a decision is made and its fate will depend on a number of things. Sales potential is a big factor; to whom will the book appeal? Will it pay for itself within a specified time? A book may be beautifully written and presented yet have limited appeal in the marketplace and as a result be turned down with regret.

Once the work is in production, a variety of editors will be involved, although on a small magazine or newspaper one person may wear several hats. Articles may be altered slightly to conform to house style; grammar and spelling errors will be tidied up. Sometimes the writer will be asked to lengthen a piece, or to tighten it up. The author may have to consider making changes to his book which, the editor feels, will make it more commercially viable. The true professional works with the editor to strengthen the work, unless he strongly disagrees with what is being asked of him.

Editors' expectations

Editors expect that you will:

- Submit a neatly typed manuscript, accompanied by sufficient postage for its return (once the work has been accepted you don't have to pay additional postage for the manuscript to be returned to you for alteration, or for proofs which you are meant to correct).

- Not arrive in person with a manuscript, or attempt to make an initial contact by phone or fax.

- Allow one to two months before checking to see what she thinks of your manuscript. Most editors have piles of material to wade through and this all takes time.

- Refrain from making demands with your initial submission, such as how much you want to be paid, or when the work should be published. It is quite acceptable to state the rights being offered.

- Work with her in a professional manner to upgrade the manuscript if necessary.

- Not quibble over every little suggestion or alteration. Save yourself for the important things.

- Accept the fact that parts of your work may be cut out. In the case of a book this should be discussed with you; your contract should state that no major alterations will be made without your approval.
  It's a different matter when it comes to newspaper and magazine articles which must fit into a certain slot on the page. Advertisements (which pay to keep the publication

going) are placed on the page first and the copy fills the remaining space. If there is one paragraph too many, it has to go. Also, there are rules to laying out pages; a lone word or line may not be carried over to the next page.

- Wherever possible, co-operate with the editor when you are asked to help with book promotion, and don't take matters into your own hands without her knowledge.

Things that make editors turn grey:

- Authors who tour book shops, demanding to know why their books aren't in stock.

- Authors who slip into shops and, unasked, sign copies of their books. As a result, vendors cannot return unsold books for credit, so this is unpopular all round.

- Writers who disagree over house style, complaining about the choice of type face, or punctuation (why isn't there a full stop after the word Mr?).

Remember: nobody has an automatic right to be published. Rock the boat too heavily and you may not be given a second chance.

You have rights too!

Are we insisting that the editor is king? No. He or she certainly wields a great amount of power, but you do have rights. If there is a personality conflict between you and your editor, or she is being totally unreasonable, you can, of course, ask to have a different one assigned to you. While this may work well for the best-selling author, where the novice is concerned it all boils down to whether to go or to stay. How badly do you want to be published?

I was once assigned to write an article for a regional magazine in which my work had been published several times before. Being the author of a book about Welsh settlement in Canada during the past 300 years, I meant to write about aspects of that history as it applied to the magazine's circulation area.

By the time the article was completed, however, the editor had left the magazine and been replaced by someone new. He asked me to make radical changes to the piece, which I did.

Having received the new manuscript he phoned up and said 'It's well written, but I've changed my mind. I want it tackled from a different angle. Write about the problems of adjustment these new immigrants experienced in the 1950's.'

That was when I decided against continuing, and politely asked to have the manuscript returned. The whole thrust of the piece had been to dispel the myth that the Welsh were part of the postwar mass migration from Europe to Canada and to underline that they had, in fact, been among the founding nations of Canada.

Furthermore, the payment offered - with no kill fee - was too small a return for the amount of work involved in producing yet another version of the piece.

Editors are not necessarily infallible. (Having been one myself I can say this without fear or favour). In a condensed version of Catherine Cookson's book, *Golden Straw*, recently published in *Good Housekeeping* in the USA, a small mistake on the part of an editor was quickly noticed by British readers. The original version reads: 'He golloped beer next door in the men-only bar.' The editor amended it to 'He would gallop to the pub to drink beer.'

Hardly earth-shattering, but readers pounce on mistakes like this and love to write critical letters to the publication.

We wonder who was at fault in the case of an article about the British royal family which was published in a Canadian magazine. Stressing the middle-class origins of Prince Edward's girl friend, Sophie Rhys Jones, the writer described her as being 'Neither aristocratic nor bottom drawer.' The editor should have known that bottom drawer is not the opposite of top drawer!

Keep in mind, then, that working with your editor is a two-way street. Mutual respect and an eagle eye for mistakes will take you far.

Agents

To misquote the words of poet Thomas Edward Brown: 'An agent is a lovesome thing, God wot!'

Do you need an agent? How and where do you find one? What will he or she do for you?

Some authors maintain that an agent is essential if their work is to be properly marketed. Others believe that they are better off on their own, without having to pay a percentage of their income to a middleman. Before you decide which approach is right for you, there are a number of factors which should be taken into account.

Many publishing houses will no longer consider unagented manuscripts. Unable or unwilling to wade through thousands of manuscripts each year, they rely on agents to do the preliminary weeding out. Even in those houses which still consider unsolicited material, manuscripts sent in by an agent usually bypass the dreaded 'slush pile' where submissions can languish for months.

Unfortunately the same economic constraints that affect publishers also have a bearing on whether an agent will take you on. Persuading a good one to enter a partnership with a new writer can often prove next to impossible.

If you can't find an agent, take heart; many published authors have achieved success by researching the market carefully and dealing directly with publishers.

If you do wish to approach an agent, here are some tips.

- First decide if what you have written is likely to appeal to an agent. He makes his living from the percentage you pay him; he cannot afford to take on clients whose work is likely to enjoy only a modest financial return.

- He may be thrilled to handle your blockbuster novel, but turn down poetry, magazine articles, local history books and academic texts, all of which apply to specialist markets.

- Do you have credentials with which to back up your application? The journalist with twenty years' experience may be well equipped to write an expose of graft in a particular industry; your collection of literary short stories has more credibility if the stories have already been published in respected magazines.

What can an experienced agent do for me?

- She will match up your manuscript with a suitable house.

- She will negotiate the best possible financial deal for you, sometimes through an auction between several publishers.

- She will scrutinise your contract and obtain the best one possible, given all the circumstances.

- She will find out what resources the publisher will commit to in terms of promotion and marketing.

- She will collect your advances and royalties, check royalty statements and tackle any problems.

All this will leave you free to write, without having to worry over the problem of selling your work and getting paid.

Finding an agent

You must find a bona fide agency. Asking your Aunt Maggie to represent you is likely to land you right in the middle of the slush pile. Editors will be sceptical of her ability and experience.

- Try networking. Do you know someone who already has an agent? Ask for an introduction.

- Consider attending writers' conferences or seminars if you know that agents will be present to meet authors.

- Consult listings in writers' handbooks and directories.

- Ask professional writers' organisations if they have a pre-screened listing. Remember to enclose a SAE for their response.

What to look for:

- Are they prepared to take on new clients?

- What sort of work do they handle? Even among agents who accept only book manuscripts, there are specialists. It's a waste of everyone's time if you contact them with work which doesn't fit their requirements.

- How do they want you to make your initial approach? A query letter only? Sample chapters and a synopsis?

- Whom do they represent? How long have they been in business? Answers to these questions tell you how successful the agency is. Steer clear of anyone who gives evasive answers.

Before signing a contract with an agency you should find out what they will do for you. Will they make multiple submissions or only approach publishers one at a time? Will they tell you about rejections received, and pass on editorial comments? How many times will they send your work out before giving up?

Under what conditions may you - or they - terminate the contract? Remember that, if you part company after your book is published, the agent will still be eligible for commission earned on royalties during the life of that book.

Agents' charges

Look into this carefully because rates of commission vary from one agency to another. In Britain, approximately two thirds of all agencies charge 10% on domestic sales with the rest taking from 12½% to 15%. A few require 20%. All these figures usually differ on foreign and subsidiary sales.

Reputable agencies rely on commissions to keep them afloat. They will do their best for the writers they represent because their own livelihood depends on sales. 10% of nothing is nothing.

Avoid agencies which charge reading fees. This practise is not illegal and arguably these agents should not be asked to work for nothing. However, there is nothing to stop an unscrupulous agent (and we are certainly not suggesting that all those who charge fees are dishonest) from taking your money and then declining to take you on. They have only to say that your work did not meet their requirements and you have no redress.

Similarly, avoid paying a signing fee. Agents have legitimate expenses, such as phone calls, faxes, photocopying and so on, but these should be deducted from your royalties later on. Before signing with an agent, find out what these charges are likely to be.

Given all these variables, which way should you jump? If you wish to take charge of your first book yourself try this approach:

- After careful research, send a well-thought out query letter to several suitable publishers. Avoid those who return unagented material unread. Those who say they don't accept unsolicited manuscripts will usually read query letters and, if interested, will ask to see your work.

- On receiving the first positive response, make your submission to that publisher, scrupulously following his rules. (You may be requested to send in a chapter, or perhaps three, as well as a synopsis of the book).

- If the book is turned down, send samples to the next publisher on your list.

- After your book has been published (and, we hope, is doing well) you can send a copy to an agent, asking for representation and he just might take you on for future books. At this stage you will already have proved yourself in his eyes. A picture is worth a thousand words!

8 EARNINGS, TAX & CONTRACTS

- Payment for articles and short stories
- Earnings from books
- Author's copies
- You and the taxman
- Allowable deductions
- Public Lending Right
- Publishing contracts
- Rights
- American markets

There is more to writing than the enjoyment of being creative and the thrill of being published. Whether your object is to earn a living from your craft or to make a little pin money from a spare-time activity, you must pay attention to the financial side of the business.

Payment for articles and short stories

How much can you expect to be paid for your work?

The remuneration for an article or short story largely depends on the size (the circulation numbers) of the periodical in which it will be printed and the length of the piece itself. It could range from a meagre £10 to a respectable fee of several hundred pounds.

This may be expressed as so many pence per word, based on the actual number used rather than in your original manuscript. Some small magazines offer a set sum per printed page; some newspapers still pay by the column inch.

Some idea of the payment offered by a particular firm might be found under their entry in a publishing directory, or in their guidelines, if they have them.

Increasingly, magazine listings indicate that 'payment is negotiable.' What exactly does this mean? Usually that they are prepared to pay more for a piece by a well-established writer or for an article they are really keen to acquire.

The amount should certainly be mentioned in their letter of acceptance. If it is not, you have the right to politely enquire. As a first-timer you may be wise to accept the remuneration that is offered, unless it is absolutely ridiculous; those who display undue greed can price themselves out of the market.

If you have supplied original illustrations to accompany an article, you could receive an additional payment for each one used. Do be clear on this; if you obtain them from a photo bank, who pays, you or the publisher? If he has to round up pictures, will the cost of these be deducted from your cheque?

The way in which payment is made varies from one publication to another. Payment on acceptance, payment on publication, payment after publication. Obviously, payment on acceptance is best; magazine editors work several months in advance of publication and your contribution may not be used for some time.

If payment is to be made upon publication, ask if you can expect a kill fee if, for some reason, your article isn't used after all. A kill fee is usually a percentage of the publication price. The least desirable option is payment after publication - perhaps 30 days later. This means that your money is tied up for some time while the publisher has the use of it. Also, there is always the possibility that you might never see it at all if he should go out of business in the meantime.

As a writer new to the publication you should accept what is on offer but if you become a regular contributor you can expect to do better in due course, or at least, like Oliver Twist, feel justified in asking for more.

Some smaller periodicals don't pay in cash at all, but offer free copies in exchange for your work. This brings us to another point: should you ever offer your services free of charge? There are times when you might.

Perhaps you could write a column or cover community events for your local newspaper, if it is a small operation which cannot afford payment. The reward here is that you collect a file of clippings to show magazine editors as proof that you have appeared in print before. (And don't send off the originals; make photocopies).

You may also decide to prepare that commemorative booklet for your church or Women's Institute without pay as your way of supporting the organisation. This, too, can be used as evidence that you have the ability to follow through on a project. However, that is as far as you should go.

Never suggest to a magazine editor that you will work

without pay in return for being published! This brands you as an amateur, stating in effect that you lack the confidence or the talent to compete with professional writers. It will also make you unpopular with your peers, struggling writers who need the money!

Earnings for books

Books are paid for in a different way. Whereas you will probably be paid a flat fee when commissioned to write a book such as the history of a corporation, when it comes to works purchased by publishers who supply the book trade you will receive royalties. A royalty is a percentage of the retail price of each book sold. The amounts vary from one publishing house to another, depending on the size of the company.

In the best scenario, an advance royalty is paid; this is a non-returnable sum which will be deducted from future earnings. You may be paid half of the promised sum upon delivery of an acceptable manuscript by a previously agreed-upon deadline and the remainder upon publication. Occasionally an advance will be paid before the book is written, usually in the case of some eagerly-sought-after commercially viable book, but this seldom happens to the novice writer.

Some small houses may not offer an advance at all and you may have to wait until your first royalty statement appears (these are usually prepared once or twice a year) to find out if you have made any money at all. You will obviously make some money by this method, but be aware that most publishers maintain a 'reserve against returns' (an average 20%) which will affect your payments. Book sellers have limited space in which to display their wares and books which do not sell within a certain period of time are returned to the publisher for credit. Although a publisher may receive advance orders for, say, 5,000 copies of your book this doesn't mean that all of them will be purchased by the public. Royalties are due only on copies for which money is actually received.

In some cases your royalty may be a percentage of the publisher's net receipts. That is, the retail price minus the trade discount which the bookseller receives.

A popular book will sometimes be sold at a discount by the big chains, a practice which is deplored by authors because it results in lower royalties. All they can do is to hope that the shortfall will be made up from the extra sales which result from this exposure.

Independent book shops will often keep local-interest titles on display for an indefinite period, which is good news for those people published by small, regional houses. In this case, royalties may well accumulate over time, balancing out the modest returns from a small press run.

If you have collaborated with a co-author, the royalties will be shared between you. If illustrations are a major part of the book, as in the case of a picture book for children, author and illustrator generally share the royalty on a 50-50 basis.

When you have an agent, he will deduct his commission from your royalty cheque before passing on the residue to you.

Author's copies

Authors receive a number of free copies when their books are first published, usually 10 or 12. Additional copies can be purchased from the publisher at a trade discount. No royalties are payable on such books because no profit accrues to the publisher. When the book is remaindered you should have the opportunity to buy more copies at a discount price, should you wish to do so.

You and the tax man

Before we leave the subject of money, be warned that you will be expected to declare for tax purposes any money that you make from your writing. Publishers do not deduct money at source. Keep a careful record of all payments made to you.

For tax purposes, you are classed as a professional if you produce written work on a regular basis with the intention of making a profit. Where does the novice writer fit into this? You may be writing every evening, certainly with the hope of being paid for your work, yet acceptances are few and far between. At this stage the Tax Inspector may label your writing as a hobby, which will affect the amount of work-related expenses you are allowed to claim.

If the day comes when you decide to make your living solely from writing, you will have to make national insurance payments as a self-employed person. If your gross annual income from writing exceeds is more than a certain amount you will be required to register for VAT.

Allowable deductions

The good news is that, as a professional writer, you can use the tools of your trade as tax deductions. Some examples follow:

- If you work out of a home office, claim a portion of your rent, rates, heating and lighting costs.

- Claim depreciation on your capital investments (typewriter, computer, desk, etc).

- Total your annual cost of stationery, postage, photocopying and work-related telephone charges.

- Travel. If a freelance assignment requires you to drive to another town to conduct an interview or do research, bus fares or petrol will be involved. Keep receipts to substantiate your claims. If, however, the person who hires you underwrites those costs, you cannot claim them as deductions.

- Periodicals and books necessary for your work.

- Any publishing-related expenses such as the cost of having an index prepared, or travelling to a meeting with your editor.

- Professional subscription fees.

If you can afford it, it may be worth your while to hire a professional accountant to deal with your tax return. There is much more to the taxation laws as applied to writers than we have space for here and he or she may be able to save you money. For instance, there are cases where you may be able to average out lump sums, or losses, over an extended period. And yes, you can chalk up the accountant's fee as another deduction.

Public Lending Right

The Public Lending Right is a system where authors are eligible to receive an annual payment when their books are borrowed by library patrons. A number of countries now use this plan although the modus operandi is not identical in each.

To qualify for the British PLR you must be resident here and be the acknowledged author of a properly printed and bound book which is offered for sale. A book can't be registered prior to publication.

Authors must register themselves for the scheme; it does not happen automatically with the publication of a book, nor can the required information be submitted by their publishers. Contrary to the practise in some countries, PLR in Britain continues to be paid for 50 years after the author's death to a designated heir.

Each year, thirty sample libraries are asked to provide information pertaining to how many times the registered books are borrowed. Based on this data, authors receive payment from the government-funded scheme. At present, more than 24,000 authors are registered; over 75% of them receive less than £100 per year. Very few people receive the maximum allowable payment of £6,000 and many receive nothing at all. The popularity of an author's books and the number of people participating in the pool have a bearing on what you will receive.

A pamphlet available from the PLR office explains which books are eligible. You must declare your PLR payment on your tax return, but you are not liable for VAT.

Publishing contracts

In her autobiography, Agatha Christie tells how she came to sign her first book contract which gave her no royalties whatsoever on the first two thousand copies sold. 'Having given up hope for some years of having anything published except the occasional short story and poem,' she wrote, 'I would have signed anything.'

No matter how thrilled you are never agree to your book being published without first signing a contract. Some of the larger periodicals also provide contracts when a large piece of work is assigned to you; most of the smaller ones do not and you will have to rely on the editor's letter to prove what your rights and obligations are. When in doubt, ask.

Read the contract that is offered to you by your publisher. Go over it with a fine tooth comb. When dealing with one for the first time, have it looked over by your solicitor. Be aware that, while he or she will be able to point out any obvious flaws or loopholes, few lawyers have much experience in the world of publishing. They may not be familiar with the ins and outs of royalties, advances, and 'rights'. The contract on page 90 is recommended by the Society of Authors.

The contract you are offered is not carved in stone. Some points may be negotiable. As a first time author you may not be in a position to ask for a larger advance but with several published books to your credit it would be reasonable to do so.

Don't promise anything that you can't deliver. Publishers plan their lists well ahead of time; if for instance you have agreed to an October deadline you must adhere to it. Book production takes several months and publishers are often on a tight schedule.

You may be asked to give the publisher first refusal on your next book or books. This is only fair. He may not expect to reap much of a return on a first book by an unknown author but takes you on in the hope that further down the road your work will develop into a paying proposition.

You will probably be asked to correct the proofs and, if

you are not, you can ask to have inserted into the contract a clause which gives you the right to at least see them. Please note that your job is to locate any typographical or factual errors that have escaped the editor's eye. This is *not* the time to make plot changes or to add an extra paragraph on page 37. All that should have been done at the manuscript stage, or at least while working with your editor on improving the product.

Each publishing company has its own in-house style. If they choose to print chapter headings in italic type or to group photographs in special sections rather than scattering them throughout the book, that is their privilege and you should not attempt to interfere.

In the case of a pictorial book ask to see the blueprint before the book goes to press, not in order to make a fuss but just to check that the pictures have been stripped into the right spots. Otherwise it would be humiliating if you were to open your brand new copy of *Women in History* to find your cherished photo of Margaret Thatcher identified as Boadicea.

You may not have any control over the cover design, but if possible ask to see the cover or jacket blurb, that short description of contents which plays a factor in whether the customer will buy the book. My first novel was set in Canada during the War of 1812 against the United States and I was totally mortified when I saw on the cover the opening statement that 'Quebec has just fallen...' a piece of history that had taken place half a century before my plot setting.

You should also be aware of the format in which your book will be published. A cloth bound or hard cover book may be followed a year later by a paperback edition. Royalties on the former will be higher because of the retail price yet sales of the latter will probably be better because more people can afford to buy them.

Mass market books, which are often paperback originals, are distributed in many different places, including supermarkets and railway station book stalls. They have a short shelf life and may not remain in print for long. On the plus side, the volume of sales may be enormous, as is the case with the various Harlequin lines.

In between the two there are quality paperbacks, attractive books which may find a permanent home on the customer's bookshelf. These are usually well-made volumes which are less expensive to produce than their cloth-bound counterparts.

The book will be classed as out of print when stocks fall below 50 hard cover or 150 paperback books. You'll want to know if the publisher will be reprinting when that time comes. If not, can you offer it elsewhere, or possibly bring out a new edition yourself? Provision for such eventualities should be included in the contract.

A standard contract should also spell out what the publisher will do for you, and what payment you can expect, in the event of book club sales, foreign sales and so on. Note that even though these eventualities may be spelled out in a contract, the publisher will not necessarily be bound to follow these avenues. A local history book for instance, is unlikely to be sold in America or made into a film.

If you have written a non-fiction book for which an index

is necessary, who pays for the services of a professional indexer if you cannot undertake the task? Will it be you, or the publisher? Leave nothing to chance.

Rights

Whether you are signing a book contract or submitting an article to a newspaper or magazine, the question of rights is important. Copyright has already been discussed; you know that you own the copyright of any written work created by you, except in the case of work for hire. The copyright holder has the sole right to reproduce a work or to permit others to do so.

This question of permission is important. When you assign first rights the buyer must be the first to publish your piece, although you retain the copyright. When you sell one time rights you are legally free to sell the article to a secondary market, but only after it has already appeared in print in the first publication.

Under reprint rights a magazine, such as Reader's Digest, may reprint a piece which has appeared elsewhere, by paying a fee to the author or the other publisher.

On purchasing serial rights, a publisher can publish a work in sister publications owned by him without paying an additional fee.

Some major publishers in both Britain and the USA, are now requesting that copyright be assigned to them. This gives them control of all aspects of the work, including reprint, translation and electronic rights. Writers' associations are warning against this system because it benefits the publisher while the hapless author does not receive payment for these additional services.

Unfortunately many writers are finding themselves in a David and Goliath situation. It is all very well to say that authors should stand firm, but those refusing to comply could well find themselves out in the cold. At the time of writing this issue is under discussion by the British government.

American markets

You probably know that many books by British authors are also published in the United States, but what about magazine articles? Do you have a chance of being published there?

The answer is yes, if you have something to say which will interest American readers. Travel articles, British history, genealogy, self help, health and fitness are all good topics if you approach them from the right angle.

In the Help List section of this book you'll find information about some of the magazines and handbooks which are published in America, invaluable to you if you plan to write for their markets. The handbooks include 'how-to' chapters - some by British writers!

9 THE SELF-PUBLISHING OPTION ?

- For and against
- Accepting the challenge
- Pricing a book
- Hiring a printer
- How many books?

As the twentieth century draws to a close an ever-increasing number of authors seem to view self-publishing as the way to go. Having faith in their work but with no luck in placing their work with trade publishers, they decide to strike out on their own. There is no law against this but there are pitfalls to be avoided. This chapter outlines some of the pros and cons.

For and against

Years ago many novice authors started out by publishing their own work. In 1901, for example, after being rejected by seven publishers, Beatrix Potter had 250 copies of The Tale of Peter Rabbit printed privately, most of which were bought by friends and relations. The book attracted favourable reviews, after which the firm of Frederick Warne, who had previously turned it down, agreed to publish a new addition. For this she received a royalty of threepence in the shilling.

She would be amazed by the amount of related memorabilia which is on the market today, many years after her death. Who would have thought that these delightful, childish tales would spawn everything from figurines of the characters to Peter Rabbit wallpaper?

In later years the idea of self-publishing came to be looked down upon by those lucky enough to have their work accepted professionally. A certain amount of snobbery was inherent in this viewpoint, the inference being that privately printed works fell short of an acceptable standard.

Now, particularly in America, the concept of producing one's own work is once again seen as a viable option, particularly in the field of local interest books. As economic downsizing continues to plague the publishing industry many books which might have had a chance of being accepted a decade or so ago, are now likely to be rejected. Thus an increasing number of authors are taking matters into their own hands, often with great success.

If you plan to follow their example, there are things that you should know before making the attempt. While your venture can certainly have a happy outcome, it pays to be aware of the inherent difficulties. The self-publisher's motto should be 'Let the Buyer Beware.' (And, it must be admitted, there are times when this should also be the watchword of the person who buys one of his books. Not everyone is cut out to be a publisher).

Subsidy publishers - also known as the vanity press - undertake to produce your work in book form for a fee.

The onus is then on you to market your work.

In recent months Britain's Advertising Standards Authority have investigated a number of complaints about certain subsidy publishers who appear to have been making exaggerated claims of what they can do for the author.

Such publishers, whose advertisements appear in quality magazines, are in business to make a profit which of course is fair enough. What is not fair is that a few unscrupulous companies make promises they have no intention of keeping, such as undertaking to distribute or advertise your books. They may encourage you to order a larger number of copies than you can hope to distribute. If your book happens to be poorly written, would they risk losing your contract by telling you so?

How do you recognise members of the vanity press? First of all, by understanding that bona fide publishers - firms who pay you rather than the other way around - do not need to advertise for manuscripts. They already have more than enough submissions to choose from. Some advertisements simply declare that a firm will publish your book, a come-on which encourages you to apply for further details. Others offer to publish as a co-partnership or joint venture, which means that they do the production work and you foot the bill.

Before taking the plunge, think twice about publishing at your own expense. Trade publishers may have turned you down because they know that the market for it is too small.

A first-time author of a novel will have great difficulty in recouping even part of his investment. Such a book needs exposure on a national level, yet how do you distribute books to every store in the British Isles? Think of the cost of production, delivery and advertising! Reviewers seldom promote self-published works.

Accepting the challenge

Let's suppose that you have tried unsuccessfully to interest a commercial publisher in your manuscript and have now decided to go the self-publishing route. Some careful research is necessary before you part with your hard-earned money.

Is there a need for a book such as yours? First investigate the market place, although we hope that you did that before submitting your manuscript to those professional editors! Go to the library and see if anyone has written a book on a similar theme. If there are already six variations on 'gardening for beginners' on the shelves, yours might not sell. On the other hand, if your idea is too narrow - a history of the local brick works, for example - there may not be a market for that, either.

Find someone who will proof read your manuscript. A subsidy publisher is unlikely to edit your work for you. Ask one or two people to give you an honest appraisal of the book (do not include your proud mother).

Before signing a contract, know exactly what you are getting for your money. Ask to see samples of other books they've produced. Ask if they'll provide you with a blue print of the book before it goes to press; this is particularly important in the case of a pictorial book because you'll want to know that pictures have been stripped into the right slot and are correctly identified.

Obtain estimates from two or three companies and compare prices. Unit costs vary according to the size of the press run so know your requirements before asking them to quote you a price. There is a saying in the trade that the first copy is the most expensive. This is because certain procedures, such as typesetting, making page negatives or setting up the press, are necessary whether you are printing one copy or ten thousand. The more copies of a book that are produced the cheaper the unit cost will be.

The type of cover will have a bearing on cost, too. Cloth bound or hard cover books are much more expensive than paperbacks, which is why so many people prefer to buy the latter. The usual method, using glue, is called Perfect Binding. Cloth books are usually stitched. A choice of spiral bindings is available for recipe books, and sometimes DIY books, which can then be opened flat, but these are never used for novels and other forms of reading material.

Don't fall into the trap of buying a larger number of books than you can reasonably expect to sell, just because the unit cost seems to be cheaper that way. The unit cost on 500 books may appear to be £5 (a very conservative estimate, used here for the purpose of easy mental arithmetic) but you won't make a profit from unsold books. If you only sell fifty the price of producing each of those has really amounted to £50 each!

Sit down with a calculator and work out the true cost of marketing the book. When you place it in a book shop, expect to allow the proprietor a trade discount of 35% or 40% of the retail price. Some people try to get away with less when pushing a local interest book but this really isn't fair to the book seller, whose living it is, and you won't find him rushing to reorder the title.

The larger chains often refuse to stock self-published books and even the smaller, independent shop may only be able to display your title for a limited time. Space is at a premium and there are always new books coming in. Professional publishers expect to see unsold books being returned to them on a regular basis, except in the case of a best-selling title.

Your book is likely to be taken on consignment, which means that the book seller can return copies for credit at any time. Books are seldom sold outright to a store, except in the case of remainders, and invoices are unlikely to be settled in less than thirty days.

If you manage to interest a distributor in your book, expect to pay him 15% or 20% of the retail price for his services. Budget an extra 2% for advertising purposes.

Pricing a book

In order to sell, your book should command a similar price to others which are similar in format. Visit a local shop and check the retail prices of books of a similar size. For easy reference, we'll say that paperbacks like yours are sold for £10. We'll call this sum 100%. Deduct the trade discount and distributor's fee, any other projected unit, costs plus 10% profit for yourself. The remaining percentage must be equal to, or less than, the unit cost of publishing.

Remember that for each pound you think of tacking on to the retail price, you will only make an additional 10p whereas the vendor will net an additional 40p. The retail price of the book may then be pushed to a level which is more than the market will bear.

You can avoid some of the above costs by distributing the book yourself, by setting up a mail order service, or by attending craft shows and sales. Bear in mind that these alternatives call for an outlay in time, petrol or advertising.

Hiring a printer

An alternative to signing with a subsidy publisher is to approach a local printer, thus cutting out the middleman. The advantages are:

- You have more control over a local business, whose owner depends on his good reputation in the community.

- Costs should be lower.

- You can ask him to keep 'long term' plates on hand so that reprints can be made more cheaply, and at relatively short notice if necessary. Once again, ask to see samples of books he has produced before.

- Ask for a firm date when your book will be ready.

Before asking for an estimate you must know how many pages will be in the book and how many copies you'll need. You must also specify the number of photographs or drawings which are to be used.

Consider paying for the services of a freelance editor or proofreader to tidy up the work before it goes to the printer. Typesetters are not required to correct mistakes other than their own.

Even more money can be saved if you can deliver camera-ready copy to the printer. This means that you, or a friend, have already made up the book pages with the help of desktop publishing software.

This should only be attempted if you are experienced in this type of work. I shall never forget the sorry spectacle of an unskilled acquaintance whose efforts left him in great difficulty. At the time, book pages were still being made up by means of applying wax to one side of computerized printouts which were then pressed on to layout sheets the size of the page. Many newspapers are still using this method.

Poor Philip, with no experience in cutting and pasting reams of type, turned up at the printer's with a box filled with pages from which strips of paper dangled in every direction. It apparently hadn't occurred to him that real books have neatly finished edges. The result was that a professional compositor had to redo the job, thereby putting up the price.

Still, problems can occur even when an author is under contract to a trade publisher. Pleased to have finished correcting the proofs of her book, my friend Jan left them in an open box while she went off to make a celebratory cup of tea. Alas, in her absence, the cat used the carton as a litter box.

How many books?

Now back to that knotty problem; how many books should you have printed, and how many can you reasonably hope to sell? A history of your parish church may sell 500 copies, whereas a how-to book which 'catches on' may sell thousands.

Here are some factors you should take into consideration.

- Is your name known to readers? Have you given lectures, or appeared in print before? Are you in the public eye in some way?

- Names sell. When I donated part of my large collection of mystery novels to the book table at the church bazaar I was surprised to see which sold and which ones I had to take home again. Far from reading the cover blurb, customers lost no time in pouncing on a Ruth Rendell or an Agatha Christie, ignoring works by some excellent American writers who were unknown to them.

Final thoughts

If you've managed to negotiate the minefield of self-publishing and have produced a fine book which has been snapped up in no time, you can use it to parlay your way to greater things. An agent or trade publisher may now be willing to take you on; you will have proved your worth. Who knows? You may even be able to sell the rights to a trade publisher who will continue to reprint and market the title under his imprint.

Another positive sign, both in Britain and America, is that some writer's magazines, seeing the increasing popularity of this member of the print family, are now offering awards for excellence in self-published books.

This should not be taken to mean that they are supporters of the vanity press.

10 WHERE TO FIND SUPPORT ?

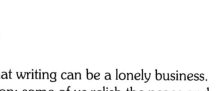

- Writing schools and courses
- Choosing a course
- Workshops, conferences and seminars
- Writers' circles
- Competitions
- Books
- Writing magazines
- Professional organisations

It has often been said that writing can be a lonely business. This is a matter of opinion; some of us relish the peace and quiet which allows the creative juices to flow and the only problem is how to achieve it!

The part-time writer has to juggle the demands of family life against writing time and it takes dedication to keep one's mind on the plot of a novel when the washing machine has overflowed or the dog is missing.

The full-time author who is able to budget larger portions of writing time faces a different problem. He or she will be expected to drop everything to talk on the phone, entertain visitors or take on volunteer service 'Because you don't work.' Or, when the telephone answering machine is left to field the calls there will be at least one plaintive message saying 'Why don't you pick up the phone? I know you're there.'

It seems that few writers have the privilege of being left alone to get on with the job. Perhaps a better way of describing the problem is that nobody seems to understand what they are up against. It does no good to explain to Aunt Julie that you simply can't down tools at a moment's notice to attend her dinner party when there are bills waiting to be paid. 'I know, dear,' she'll say, sweetly. 'Why don't you get a proper job?'

The novice often feels the lack of the positive feed-back that the established writer takes for granted. Enthusiastic reviews and fan mail are confidence builders, but when you are still at the stage where rejection slips arrive with depressing regularity it's easy to give way to self-doubt.

The good news is that nobody needs to soldier on alone. There is plenty of help out there if you choose to take it. Writing schools and courses can put you on the right track; workshops and conferences build enthusiasm; writers' circles put you in touch with like-minded people; competitions spur you on; professional organisations assist with day-to-day problems. Magazines and specialist books abound.

Writing schools and courses

You may wonder why this subject is being discussed near the end of the book. Wouldn't it have made more sense to place it at the very beginning?

There are two reasons for this. First of all, it's quite possible to become a successful writer without ever having taken a writing course. Many people have done so in the past. A case in point is Sir Winston Churchill, a brilliant man who, although he did badly at school, went on to achieve greatness. While he is best remembered as the Prime Minister who led Britain through the dark years of the Second World War he had an early career as a journalist and later published a number of books.

The only person who can truly make a successful writer out of you is you, yourself. You can be taught the mechanics of the craft but no outsider can give you the talent, the self-discipline and the ideas that will lift you above the crowd.

Having said this, we acknowledge that courses can be of tremendous benefit along the way. Here are some of the reasons:

- Some people learn best from practical, hands-on methods.

- Attending class encourages you to pay attention to your craft on a regular basis. Talent can be nurtured through regular application to detail.

- You learn to work to deadlines.

- Qualified instructors suggest how your work might be improved. An article or story which is beautifully written and grammatically correct may still be unmarketable.

- You gain confidence as your body of work grows.

- Specialist courses, such as fiction-writing, can help even the established writer; styles and requirements do vary from one branch of writing to another. Many of today's published novelists started out as newspaper reporters. When they switched fields they had to learn to adapt their style from the terse prose required by newspapers to meet the demands of fiction writing technique, with plot, dialogue and characterisation.

- Some disciplines require specialised training. Very different rules govern the preparation and presentation of poetry and plays or scriptwriting. You perhaps studied poems at school and could toss off a sonnet with the best of them, but is that what interests editors today? What do you know about haiku, tanka, free verse?

Any weekly newspaper editor will tell you how much he dreads seeing the doggerel that crosses his desk from time to time, submitted by readers hoping to see their work in print. These verse-makers (we won't call them poets) regard poetry as the easiest medium in the craft of writing, while in reality it is one of the most demanding.

Scriptwriting also call for specific skills. Whether you wish to write for television, radio or the stage you must learn the basics.

Choosing a course

The type of course you take will depend very much on what you can afford, where you live and how much time you have to spare. Some colleges and universities offer credit courses, even degrees, in creative writing; others provide non-credit courses for self-improvement. Evening classes may be offered in your town. A good place to start looking is your public library; they should be able to tell you what is on offer.

Correspondence courses are also available. These range all the way from creative writing options in schools which deal in many subjects, to specialist training given through the home study courses run by *Writers News*. These enable you to work in the comfort of your own home, often at your own pace, and are ideal for people whose working hours are irregular.

In choosing a course, look carefully at what is offered before you sign on. Compare costs. Can you resign without penalty if you decide not to continue? Are there hidden costs, such as an additional fee or deposit for text books or audio tapes? Can you afford to buy any necessary equipment such as a typewriter or word processor? It is unlikely that hand written assignments will be accepted.

How much will it cost you to travel to class? Will you have to pay for baby-sitters on class night? Postage, to send assignments to a correspondence school instructor?

A good course may be well worth any sacrifice that you have to make. It will stretch your mind, provide you with new information and boost confidence. Avoid any organisations that make exaggerated claims (make £10,000 worth of sales in your first year with us!). If asked to sign a contract, read the small print carefully.

Workshops, conferences and seminars

These are short-term gatherings which may last from a few hours to several days. Often based on a theme - general fiction writing, historical novels, mystery and suspense - they may be held in a church hall, a residential centre or be part of an exotic holiday in a foreign country. Established or 'name' writers form a panel of experts.

Before signing up for such a workshop, make sure that it will meet your own particular needs. Some consist mainly of talks given by the experts, others allow you to read aloud from your own work-in-progress and receive the criticism from the instructor or your fellow participants. Is time scheduled for you to have a one-on-one discussion with one or more of the course leaders?

Writers' circles

These are fast gaining popularity in the British Isles today. They can range from a small group of friends who meet informally to discuss their work and discuss their problems to the well-organised circle of people who meet on a regular basis and who perhaps publish collections of their work.

Each have their merits. The key to success here is 'small is beautiful.' When a circle becomes too large it becomes difficult to give adequate attention to the work of each member.

If there is no writers' circle in your district, start one up. There is no law against it! Find listings in writers' directories and magazines.

Competitions

An astonishing number of competitions are offered to writers in Britain these days. Why should you enter any of these?

- It's a nice, anonymous, way to begin sending out your stories and articles. While you may not win, no nasty rejection is likely to result.

- You learn to meet deadlines.

- It's good training in learning to work on an assigned theme.

- It provides good experience in preparing and sending out a manuscript; those who ignore the rules have their entries eliminated early on.

- If you win a high-profile competition, (particularly in novel writing, such as the annual Catherine Cookson prize) you are sure to attract the attention of publishers and agents.

Writing Magazine, *Writers News* and *Writers' Monthly* regularly run competitions. The winners see their work in print, along with the judge's critique. Some book publishers, and several magazines, have recently held competitions in order to promote new talent.

Some writing competitions require that a fee be included with your entry.

Books

The aspiring writer should build a library of books related

to the craft. There are many good ones on the market today, each dealing with a separate aspect of writing, such as poetry, scriptwriting, mystery, plots, historical novels and so on.

Writing magazines

No writer, even the most experienced, should be without a subscription to a good writing magazine. If you're not sure which one would suit you best, read a few issues first. Find them in the library, at your news agent's or write to the publisher. He or she will be happy to sell you an individual copy if you send a cheque or money order for the cover price plus postage.

Some of the benefits of writing magazines are:

- They print useful 'how-to' articles.

- They often include interesting profiles of, or interviews with, famous writers. It's interesting to see how these 'greats' made it to the top of the tree.

- They discuss common errors of grammar and style.

- They advertise just about everything of interest to a writer: courses, workshops, books, directories, writers' circles, typing services, secluded cottages for rent!

- They often include reviews of books meant for writers.

- Competitions, problem-solving departments, letters to the editor are all grist to the writer's mill.

- You receive the latest news of what is happening in the markets. Although there are several excellent directories available to the writer they do not include every publisher in the country. Some companies prefer not to be listed, perhaps because they are habitually swamped with submissions and choose not to invite more.

Changes can occur among those who are listed; there is a certain amount of turnover, especially in the magazine trade. New publications start up. Established ones change direction, go out of business or no longer accept unsolicited material. Directories cannot list these changes until the following year whereas writing magazines can disseminate the information within a month.

- Writing magazines can inspire you.

Professional organisations

There are a number of professional organisations for writers in Britain. Membership in some cases is limited to published writers who meet certain qualifications. However, these organisations benefits us all, by:

- Working for minimum standards in the industry.

- Arbitrating disputes between members and publishers.

- Providing legal advice to members.

- Alerting members to any unfair dealing by publishers.

Dedicated work by such groups has resulted in the introduction of the Public Lending Right.

HELP LIST

- Societies and Associations
- Magazines
- Magazines U.S.A.
- Reference books
- Reference books U.S.A.
- Other useful addresses

Societies and Associations

The Society Of Authors
84 Drayton Gardens
London SW10 9SB
Tel 0171 373 6642

The Writer's Guild Of
Great Britain
430 Edgware Road
London W2 1EH
Tel 0171 723 8074

National Council For
The Training Of
Journalists (NCTJ)
Carlton House
Hemnall, Epping
Essex CM16 4NL
Tel 01378 72395

National Union Of
Journalists (NUJ)
Acorn House
314 Gray's Inn Road
London WC1X 8DP
Tel 0171 278 7916

The Friends Of
Arvon Foundation
6 Church Street
Darfield
Yorkshire S73 9LG

Society Of Women
Writers & Journalists
110 Whitehall Road
Chingford
London E4 6DW

The Penman Club
185 Daws Heath Road
Benfleet
Essex SS7 2TF
Tel 01702 557 431

The Newspaper
Society Training Dept
Whitefriars House
Carmelite Street
London EC4Y 0BL
Tel 0171 583 3311

Poetry Now
1-2 Wainman Road
Woodston
Peterborough PE2 7BU
Tel 01733 230746

Arrival Press
1-2 Wainman Road
Woodston
Peterborough PE2 7BU
Tel 01733 230762

Arts Councils and Regional Arts Boards

The Arts Council Of
England
14 Great Peter Street
London SW1P 3NQ
Tel 0171 333 0100

The Arts Council Of
Ireland
70 Merrion Square
Dublin 2
Tel 00 353 1 6611840

The Arts Council Of
Northern Ireland
185 Stranmillis Road
Belfast BT9 5DU
Tel 01232 381591

Scottish Arts Council
12 Manor Place
Edinburgh EH3 7DD
Tel 0131 226 6051

The Arts Council Of
Wales
Museum Place
Cardiff CF1 3NX
Tel 01222 394711

English Regional Arts
Boards
5 City Road
Winchester
Hampshire SO23 8SD
Tel 01962 851063

Cleveland Arts
7-9 Eastbourne Road
Linthorpe, Middlesbrough
Cleveland TS5 6QS
Tel 01642 812288

East Midlands Arts
Mountfields House
Epinal Way, Loughborough
Leicestershire LE11 0QE
Tel 01509 218292

Eastern Arts Board
Cherry Hinton Hall
Cambridge CB1 4DW
Tel 01223 215355

London Arts Board
Elme House
3rd Floor, 133 Long Acre
London WC2E 9AF
Tel 0171 240 1313

North West Arts Board
4th Floor, 12 Harter Street
Manchester M1 8AS
Tel 0161 228 3062

Northern Arts Board
9-10 Osbourne Terrace
Jesmond
Newcastle Upon Tyne
NE2 1NZ
Tel 0191 281 6334

South East Arts Board
10 Mount Ephraim
Tunbridge Wells
Kent TN4 8AS
Tel 01892 515210

South West Arts Board
Bradninch Place
Gandy Street, Exeter
Devon EX4 3LS
Tel 01392 218188

Southern Arts
13 St Clement Street
Winchester
Hampshire SO23 9DQ
Tel 01962 855099

West Midlands Arts
82 Granville Street
Birmingham, B1 2LH
Tel 0121 631 3121

Yorkshire &
Humberside Arts
21 Bond Street
Dewsbury
West Yorkshire WF13 1AY
Tel 01924 455555

Magazines

Writers News
Box 4, Nairn
Scotland IV12 4HU

Writing Magazine
Box 4, Nairn
Scotland IV12 4HU

Writer's Monthly
29 Turnpike Lane
London N8 OEP
Tel 0181 342 8879

The Author
84 Drayton Gardens
London SW10 9SB
Tel 0171 373 6642

Poetry Now Magazine
1-2 Wainman Road
Woodston
Peterborough PE2 7BU
Tel 01733 230746

Rhyme Arrival
1-2 Wainman Road
Woodston
Peterborough PE2 7BU
Tel 01733 230762

Chapman
4 Broughton Place
Edinburgh EH1 3RX
Tel 0131 557 2207

Freelance Writing
& Photography
113 Abbotts Ann Down
Andover
Hampshire SP11 7BX
Tel 0126 4710701

The Freelance
NUJ Acorn House
314 Gray's Inn Road
London WC1X 8DP
Tel 0171 278 7916

Springboard -
Writing To Succeed
30 Orange Hill Road
Prestwich
Manchester M25 1LS
Tel 0161 773 5911

Panurge
Crooked Holme Farm Cottage
Brampton
Cumbria CA8 2AT
Tel 016977 41087

Magazines - U.S.A.

Writers Digest (sub dept)
PO Box 2124
Harlam
Iowa 51593-2313
USA

Writers Digest (editorial)
1507 Dana Avenue
Cincinnati
Ohio 45207
USA

The Writer
120 Boylston Street
Boston
Massachusetts 02116-4615
USA

Reference Books

Writers' &
Artists' Yearbook
(annual)
Published by A & C Black
35 Bedford Row
London WC1R 4JH

The Writer's
Handbook (annual)
Published by Macmillan
45 Islington Park Street
London N1 1QB

The Small Press Guide
(annual)
7-11 Kensington High Street
London W8 5NP

Reference Books U.S.A.

The Writer's
Handbook (annual)
Published by The Writer
(see magazine listings)

The Writer's
Market (annual)
Published by Writers Digest
(see magazine listings)

Other Useful Addresses

Public Lending Right
The Registrar
PLR Office, Bayheath House
Prince Regent Street
Stockton On Tees
Cleveland TS18 1DF

Legal Deposit Office
The British Library
Boston Spa
West Yorkshire LS23 7BY

Book Trust
Book House
45 East Hill
London SW18 2QZ

Freelance Press Services
Cumberland House
Lissadel Street
Salford
Manchester M6 6GG

Oriel (The Welsh
Arts Council Bookshop)
Oriel Bookshop
The Friary
Cardiff CF1 4AA

The Garret (Writer's Books
Mail Order)
9 High Street
Warwick CV34 4AR
Tel (01926) 492904

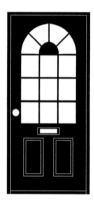